NATIONS OF THE WORLD

GERMANY

Greg Nickles and Niki Walker

www.raintreepublishers.co.uk
Visit our website to find out more information about Raintree books.

To order:
 Phone 44 (0) 1865 888113
 Send a fax to 44 (0) 1865 314091
 Visit the Raintree bookshop at www.raintreepublishers.co.uk to browse our catalogue and order online.

First published in Great Britain by Raintree, Halley Court, Jordan Hill, Oxford, OX2 8EJ, part of Harcourt Education Ltd.
Raintree is a registered trademark of Harcourt Education Ltd.

Produced for Raintree by the Brown Reference Group plc
Project Editors: Robert Anderson and Peter Jones
Designer: Joan Curtis
Cartographers: Colin Woodman and William Le Bihan
Picture Researcher: Brenda Clynch
Indexer: Indexing Specialists

Raintree Publishers
Editors: Isabel Thomas and Kate Buckingham

Printed and bound in Singapore.

ISBN 1 844 21474 5
07 06 05 04 03
10 9 8 7 6 5 4 3 2 1

British Library Cataloguing-in-Publication Data

Nickles, Greg, 1969–
    Germany – (Nations of the world)
    1. Human geography – Germany – Juvenile literature
    2. Germany – Geography – Juvenile literature
    I.Title II. Walker, Niki, 1972–
    914.3

A full catalogue is available for this book from the British Library.

Front cover: man in an Oktoberfest parade
Title page: interior of the Reichstag dome, Berlin

The acknowledgements on page 128 form part of this copyright page.

Contents

Foreword

Since ancient times, people have gathered together in communities where they could share and trade resources and strive to build a safe and happy environment. Gradually, as populations grew and societies became more complex, communities expanded to become nations – groups of people who felt sufficiently bound by a common heritage to work together for a shared future.

Land has usually played an important role in defining a nation. People have a natural affection for the landscape in which they grew up. They are proud of its natural beauties – the mountains, rivers and forests – and of the towns and cities that flourish there. People are proud, too, of their nation's history – the shared struggles and achievements that have shaped the way they live today.

Religion, culture, race and lifestyle, too, have sometimes played a role in fostering a nation's identity. Often, though, a nation includes people of different races, beliefs and customs. Many may have come from distant countries. Nations have rarely been fixed, unchanging things, either territorially or racially. Throughout history, borders have changed, often under the pressure of war, and people have migrated across the globe in search of a new life or because they are fleeing from oppression or disaster. The world's nations are still changing today: some nations are breaking up and new nations are forming.

The culture of the German people goes back many hundreds of years, but the country itself is relatively new, becoming a nation state only in 1871. Since then, Germany has undergone a turbulent history, with the negative aspects of the **Nazi** period and of two world wars. After World War Two, the country was split in half and it was only in 1990 that East Germany and West Germany were united in one state. Since reunification, however, the country has regained its place at the centre of Europe, through its role in the European Union and its extraordinary economic prowess. At the beginning of the 21st century, Germany is one of the most tolerant and prosperous nations in the world.

Introduction

Situated in the heart of central Europe, Germany borders nine countries – more than any other nation in Europe. To the north lies Denmark, and to the west the Netherlands, Belgium, Luxembourg and France. Switzerland and Austria are Germany's southern neighbours, and the Czech **Republic** and Poland lie to the east. Germany also has two stretches of coastline – on the North Sea in the north-west of the country and on the Baltic Sea in the north-east.

Germany encompasses a broad range of landscapes – from sandy beaches to lush river valleys to the majestic, snowy peaks of the Alps. A good deal of the country is covered with forests, the best-known example being the Black Forest. These woods and other natural areas are well marked with paths for walkers and cyclists, and by law even privately owned stretches of forest are available for all to enjoy.

A federal nation comprising sixteen states, Germany has its capital in Berlin. The head of state is the president, but he or she does not govern the country. The federal government is run by the chancellor and his or her ministers. Each state also has its own government, ministers and local equivalent of the chancellor. The powerful state governments can pass laws on all issues except those that affect Germany as a whole, such as foreign affairs, defence and finance.

Germany has a rich heritage. These medieval buildings are in Meersburg, a town on the Bodensee (Lake Constance) in the south of the country.

Germany's eagle

Germany's most recognized symbol is the eagle. This proudest of birds has long been associated with illustrious periods in the country's history. First appearing as the symbol of ancient Roman emperors, the eagle was later adopted as Germany's coat of arms by the German emperors who ruled the Holy Roman empire.

When Germany united in 1871, the eagle was chosen for the country's coat of arms, and in 1919 became the nation's seal. Overshadowed by the swastika during the **Nazi** period (1933–45), the symbol was readopted in 1950 by the Federal Republic of Germany (the former West Germany) as an attempt to restore German tradition and history.

The national flag of Germany consists of equal horizontal stripes of black, red and gold.

Before the single currency of the European Union (the euro) was adopted as the national currency in 2002, Germany's currency was the Deutschmark.

Germany's character has been shaped in part by its tumultuous history and shifting borders. Its many lands and peoples have belonged to a number of Europe's major empires, but no ruler united them into a single German nation until 1871. Following World War Two (1939–45), the country was split into West Germany and **communist**-controlled **East Germany**. With the fall of the Berlin Wall and many eastern European communist governments in November 1989, Germany was reunified in October 1990.

Before unification in 1871, Germany was a patchwork of loosely bound kingdoms, duchies (areas ruled by dukes), bishoprics (areas ruled by bishops) and free cities inhabited by German peoples. Peoples such as the Franks, Saxons, Bavarians and Swabians developed their own customs in each region. These tradi-

tions stayed intact while the nation was being formed and are still alive today. In a spirit of good-natured rivalry, Germans from one area often portray people from other regions as stereotypes. For example, natives of the Rhineland are characterized as relaxed and carefree, Saxons as hard working and Swabians as frugal.

PEOPLE AND LANGUAGE

After Russia, Germany has the largest population in Europe. With 82 million people sharing German soil, the country has a population density of 235 people per square kilometre (609 people per square mile), the fifth highest density in Europe. The population density is lower in the former East

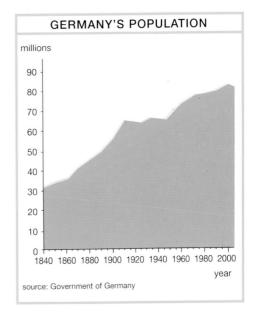

GERMANY'S POPULATION

source: Government of Germany

Germany's population is set to decrease in the future.

POPULATION DENSITY

The state with the highest density is North Rhine-Westphalia, which lies in the far west of the country with many of Germany's major cities lying along the Rhine River. The eastern state of Mecklenburg-Lower Pomerania, which borders Poland and the Baltic Sea, has the lowest population density.

Hamburg

BERLIN

Bonn

PERSONS	
Per sq km	Per sq mile
100	260
150	390
500	1290
2000	5200

Large numbers of people live in the industrialized cities of western Germany, while the south is more agricultural.

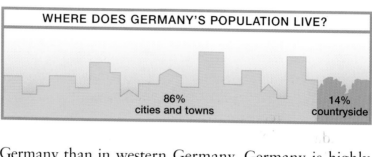

WHERE DOES GERMANY'S POPULATION LIVE?

86% cities and towns

14% countryside

With 15.5 per cent of people over 65, Germany has one of the oldest populations in the world.

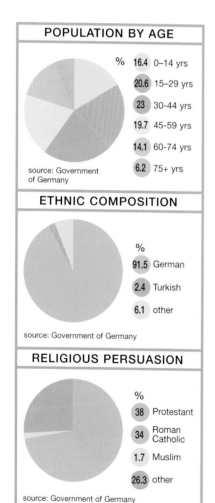

POPULATION BY AGE

%	
16.4	0–14 yrs
20.6	15–29 yrs
23	30–44 yrs
19.7	45–59 yrs
14.1	60–74 yrs
6.2	75+ yrs

source: Government of Germany

ETHNIC COMPOSITION

%	
91.5	German
2.4	Turkish
6.1	other

source: Government of Germany

RELIGIOUS PERSUASION

%	
38	Protestant
34	Roman Catholic
1.7	Muslim
26.3	other

source: Government of Germany

Germany than in western Germany. Germany is highly urbanized – about 86 per cent of its people live in cities.

The vast majority of people – 91.5 per cent – are of German origin. People who are of **Alpine** origin (originally from the Alps) live mainly in central and southern Germany, and people of Teutonic origin (from the German plains) are more concentrated in the north. Of the 7.2 million immigrants who live in Germany, the largest group is Turkish. Other groups include Italians, Greeks, Portuguese, Poles and Sorbs (see page 22). In recent years, refugees from former communist countries in eastern Europe have also flooded into Germany.

The population is mainly Christian, divided almost equally between **Protestants** and **Roman Catholics**. Northern areas tend to be mainly Protestant, while Catholicism dominates the south. German Protestants are generally called Lutherans, after the founder of Protestantism, Martin Luther (1483–1546). The next largest religion is Sunni Islam, practised mainly by the Turkish population. There are 54,000 **Jews** living in modern Germany, many in Berlin.

German language, culture and heritage extend well beyond Germany's borders. Communities of German speakers are found in Austria, the Czech Republic, the Netherlands, Russia, Switzerland, Ukraine and in other eastern European countries, such as Poland. In Germany, the German language is spoken by almost everyone. The standard language is called High German. In the regions, there are dialects that can differ quite a lot from High German. For example, Low German, spoken in the north, is more closely related to Dutch than to High German. The Sorbs – descendants of Slavic tribes called the Wends – are a large minority that speaks a language other than German. About 60,000 Sorbs live in Germany (see page 22), mainly in the east, close to the Czech and Polish borders. The Sorbish language and culture are related to those of the Czechs and Slovaks.

Germans enjoy one of the world's highest standards of living – the measure of a nation's quality of life based on life expectancy, living space, health care, diet and education. They do so mainly because of the country's strong economy, which is the third largest in the world, after the USA and Japan. In general, Germans are well educated, have a generous system of social security and are able to afford the latest consumer goods, such as cars, household appliances and computers.

Historians trace the name 'Germany' to the Romans, who explored the outlying areas of present-day Germany about 2000 years ago. The Romans encountered northern European tribes and called them the Germani, as well as naming the area Germania. In English, the name became permanently associated with the area and its peoples. The Germans call their country Deutschland.

The national anthem

Germany's national anthem, 'Deutschlandlied' ('Germany's Song'), was adopted in 1922. It is a verse of the poem 'Lied der Deutschen' ('Song of the Germans'), written in 1841 by Hoffmann von Fallersleben (1789–1874), and is set to music composed by Joseph Haydn (1732–1809) in 1797. The English translation is as follows:

Unity and rights and freedom for the German Fatherland,
Let us all pursue this brotherly purpose, with heart and hand.
Unity and rights and freedom are the pledge of happiness.
Flourish in this blessing's glory, flourish German Fatherland.

Land and cities

'Germany, unlike more fortunate countries, has no natural frontiers.'

Historian Golo Mann

Ranging from coastal mudflats and fjords in the north to the Alps mountain range in the south, Germany is an ancient land shaped not only by nature but also by centuries of human settlement. Outside its many cities and vast **industrial** regions, Germany's countryside is dotted with farms, villages and towns. Although about one-third of Germany is covered with woodland, the country has almost no wilderness. Even 'natural' areas, such as dense conifer forests, are often the result of careful human planning.

More than half of Germany's land has been adapted to agricultural use. The major farming products are cereal crops, potatoes, sugar beet, dairy produce and meat, but Germany also makes wine. The country lies just on the northern limit at which it is possible to grow and ripen wine-producing grapes. The vineyards are clustered along the Rhine and its tributaries, from just below Bonn southwards to the shores of the Bodensee (Lake Constance).

Almost all the remaining land is given over to cities and industry. Germany has twelve cities of 500,000 or more inhabitants, accounting for almost one-sixth of the entire population. Of these twelve cities, no fewer than four – Essen, Dortmund, Düsseldorf and Duisburg – are part of the huge industrial complex based on the Ruhr and Rhine rivers in the west of Germany.

Southern Germany is a land of steep mountain ranges, thick forests and clear lakes. It includes large areas with little human settlement.

FACT FILE

- Germany's largest lake is the Bodensee (Lake Constance). It is 72 km (45 miles) by 16 km (10 miles) at its longest and widest and has an area of 539 sq km (208 sq miles).

- Bavaria is the largest German state, with an area of 70,168 sq km (27,092 sq miles). The city-state of Bremen is the smallest, at 404 sq km (156 sq miles).

- Germany's agriculture is among the most efficient in the world. It is Europe's largest producer of beef, butter, milk, pork and eggs. Only about 1% of the economy, however, is dependent on agriculture.

GEOGRAPHICAL REGIONS

Germany is divided into three major geographical regions: the North German Plain, the Central Uplands and the South German Highlands. These regions stretch across the country in bands from west to east. The height above sea level increases as one travels southwards from the Baltic or North Sea coasts.

Germany's coastline fringes the North German Plain. There, the land is very flat and often rolls straight into the sea. The Baltic coast, shown here, is characterized by windswept dunes and sandy beaches.

The North German Plain

The North German Plain is a gently rolling region that averages less than 100 metres (330 feet) above sea level. It is Germany's largest geographical region, occupying the northern half of the country. The area was shaped during the last ice age, when glaciers covered almost all the land. As the ice sheets retreated, they left behind large deposits of gravel, sand and clay, creating soils that are too poor for growing most crops. Much of the plain was once covered by scrubby heath, but today it is used as grazing land for livestock or tree plantations for forestry.

The North German Plain has also been shaped by five large rivers – the Aller, Elbe, Ems, Oder and Weser – all of which flow through the plain on their way to the North or Baltic seas. Over thousands of years, these

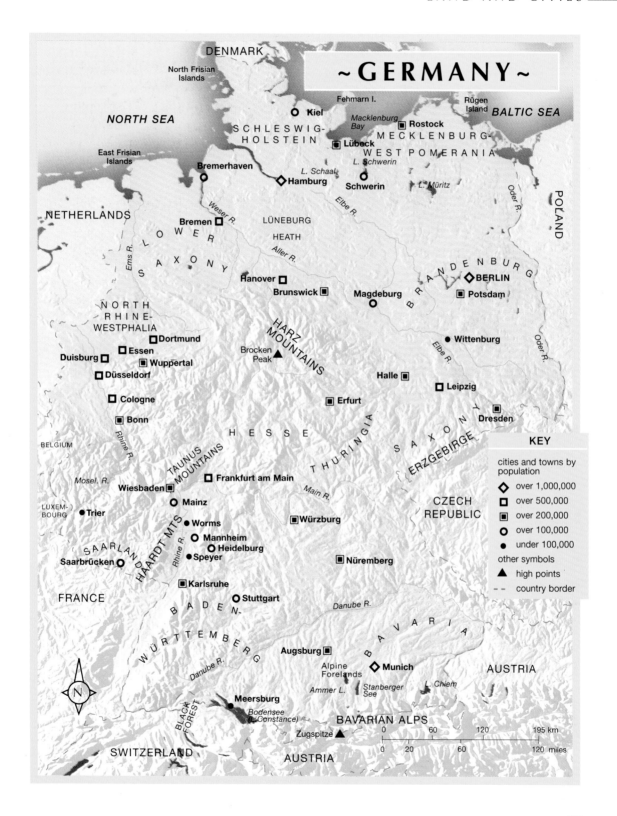

~GERMANY~

DENMARK

North Frisian Islands

NORTH SEA

Fehmarn I.

Rügen Island

BALTIC SEA

Kiel

SCHLESWIG-HOLSTEIN

Macklenburg Bay

Rostock

MECKLENBURG-WEST POMERANIA

Lübeck

L. Schwerin

East Frisian Islands

Bremerhaven

Hamburg

L. Schaal

Schwerin

L. Müritz

Oder R.

POLAND

NETHERLANDS

Weser R.

Elbe R.

Bremen

LÜNEBURG

HEATH

L O W E R S A X O N Y

Ems R.

Aller R.

Hanover

Brunswick

Magdeburg

B R A N D E N B U R G

BERLIN

Potsdam

N O R T H R H I N E - WESTPHALIA

HARZ MOUNTAINS

Brocken Peak

Elbe R.

Oder R.

Wittenburg

Dortmund

Essen

Duisburg

Wuppertal

Düsseldorf

Halle

Leipzig

Cologne

Erfurt

Dresden

Bonn

BELGIUM

H E S S E

THURINGIA

S A X O N Y

ERZGEBIRGE

Rhine R.

TAUNUS MOUNTAINS

Mosel R.

Frankfurt am Main

CZECH REPUBLIC

LUXEM-BOURG

Wiesbaden

Mainz

Main R.

Würzburg

Trier

Worms

HAARDT MTS

Mannheim

Heidelburg

Rhine R.

Speyer

Nüremberg

SAARLAND

Saarbrücken

Karlsruhe

FRANCE

B A D E N -

Stuttgart

Danube R.

W Ü R T T E M B E R G

B A V A R I A

Augsburg

Danube R.

Alpine Forelands

Munich

AUSTRIA

N

Ammer L.

Stanberger See

L. Chiem

BLACK FOREST

Meersburg

Bodensee (L. Constance)

BAVARIAN ALPS

Zugspitze

SWITZERLAND

AUSTRIA

KEY

cities and towns by population

◇ over 1,000,000

□ over 500,000

■ over 200,000

○ over 100,000

● under 100,000

other symbols

▲ high points

-- country border

0   60   120   195 km

0   20   60   120 miles

GERMANY'S LANDFORMS

North German Plain
This is Germany's largest geographical region, making up the northern half of the country. With an average altitude of 100 metres (330 feet) above sea level, it has been shaped by the movement of glaciers and the flow of some of Europe's great rivers. The region is fringed by the North and Baltic seas and is extensively farmed, used mainly as grazing land.

Central Uplands
This is a region of plateaux up to 762 metres (2500 feet) above sea level and small mountains that rise to more than 914 metres (3000 feet). Steep river gorges and dense conifer forests are also characteristic features. The region is home to the Harz, Taunus and Erzgebirge mountains.

South German Highlands
Watched over by Zugspitze, Germany's highest peak, this region climbs southwards from the pastures of the Alpine Forelands into the Alps. Rising in the mysterious Black Forest, the Danube River heads through the highlands and into Austria.

rivers have carved out broad, fertile valleys. These valleys are home to many farms as well as some of the country's oldest towns and cities.

The northern coast is divided into two parts by the Jutland Peninsula. The North Sea coast has tidal flats, while the Baltic coast has long inlets, called fjords, cut into it, with peninsulas and sandy beaches.

The Rhine's modern name derives from its Latin name _Rhenus_. For the Germans, the river is 'der Rhein', for the French, 'le Rhin' and for the Dutch, 'Rijn'.

The Central Uplands

A series of rocky plateaux called the Central Uplands stretches across the middle of Germany. The landscape of this region features flat plains averaging between 305 and 762 metres (1000 and 2500 feet) above sea level, as well as steep river gorges and small mountains that rise gently from the plateaux.

Two major rivers, the Rhine (see box opposite) and the Elbe, wind their way through the Central Uplands. The narrow, deep valleys cut by these rivers are famous for their beauty. These valleys also enable roads and

The Rhine

The Rhine is one of Europe's great rivers and holds a special place in Germany's culture and economy. The Rhine's two headstreams rise high up in the Alps in southern Switzerland. These headstreams join to form the Rhine, which then flows down into the Bodensee (Lake Constance).

On its journey northwards, the Rhine first passes across a broad flood plain. Once the river flowed in great loops, but since the 19th century, engineers have gradually straightened its course to make it more accessible to shipping.

At Mainz, the Rhine is joined by the waters of the Main River and flows north-west through a deep valley surrounded by mountains. Turreted castles tower above the river (see below), while vineyards carpet the gentler slopes.

Further north-west, at Bonn, the river flows through a broad, industrialized lowland known as the Rhineland.

Here, there are busy ports and cities, and striking, modern bridges span the river. The Rhine leaves Germany at Emmerich, from where it flows roughly westwards through the Netherlands. There the river breaks up into a number of branches before reaching the sea.

The Rhine has been an important boundary between nations, but it has also helped to tie different peoples together. Since ancient times, people have travelled along the river in order to trade, and the river was an important link between southern and northern Europe. Since the Treaty of Vienna of 1815, the river has belonged to no one country and has been open to international shipping. Today, a canal links the Rhine and the Rhône in France, thus connecting the North Sea with the Mediterranean. Towns and cities of different nations on either bank of the river co-operate to develop a local, transnational region.

The Erzgebirge

The Erzgebirge (Ore Mountains) mountain range got its name because of the large deposits of minerals found there. The mountains sit along Germany's south-eastern border with the Czech Republic and have been mined since the 14th century. Originally, miners dug for iron and silver. Today, a wide range of minerals is excavated, including uranium, copper, lead and brown coal (lignite). The Ore Mountains are also home to toy-making and lace-making industries.

In the past, France has claimed the Rhine as its natural eastern border, and France and Germany went to war several times over lands to the west of the river.

At about 2850 kilometres (1770 miles) long, the Danube is Europe's second-longest river after the Volga in Russia.

railways to be built through otherwise impenetrable rugged hills. The Rhine is the busiest and best-known river in Germany. Beginning in Switzerland, the Rhine flows 1320 kilometres (820 miles) north through western Germany and the Netherlands before emptying into the North Sea. It forms part of Germany's border with Switzerland and France.

The Elbe River rises in the Czech **Republic** and flows into the North Sea at Cuxhaven some 1170 kilometres (725 miles) away. The river was once part of the border between the former **East** and **West Germany**.

The most important mountain ranges in the Central Uplands are the Harz, Taunus and Erzgebirge mountains (see box). Despite the cold winds that blow south across the North German Plain, the Harz Mountains are a popular holiday resort. Peaks in this mountain range and in the neighbouring Thuringian Forest are more than 914 metres (3000 feet) high.

The Central Uplands have thick conifer forests, which blanket valleys, mountains and hillsides. Except for a few fertile areas, mainly in river valleys, most of the land is rocky and unsuitable for growing crops.

The South German Highlands

The South German Highlands, a region of meadowed **foothills** and jagged, densely forested mountains, rise south of the Central Uplands. The highlands are home to the Danube, the only major river in Germany that flows eastwards. Rolling foothills, called the **Alpine** Forelands, extend southwards from the Danube, gradually rising to Europe's great mountain range, the Alps. Once covered by long grasses and wildflowers, most of the Alpine Forelands have been converted to pastures or fields for growing wheat and other cereal crops.

Germany's highest peak, Zugspitze, stands at 2963 metres (9721 feet) in the far south of the country in the Bavarian Alps – the branch of the Alps that extends into Germany. Mountains in the Bavarian Alps average more than 1829 metres (6000 feet) in height. Among their rocky slopes and snow-capped peaks lie clear glacial lakes fed by waterfalls and mountain streams. The Alps span the borders of several countries besides Germany, including Austria, Switzerland, Italy and France.

The Black Forest (Schwarzwald), in the south-west of the highlands, is studded with mountain peaks, some of which reach heights of more than 1219 metres (4000 feet). Between these peaks are deep, narrow valleys. The Black Forest has a reputation for ancient magic and has been the setting for many legends and folktales. It is named after its dense stands of spruce and fir trees.

The Alps extend along Germany's southern border with Austria and are a popular destination for tourists. Among Germany's most famous winter sports resorts is Berchtesgaden, situated in the Alps in the extreme south-east of the country.

Some of the political units into which Germany was once organized were called electorates. They were ruled by electors, who had the right to choose the German kings.

THE GERMAN *LÄNDER*

In the course of its long and complex history, the area of present-day Germany has been organized and reorganized into hundreds of political units. Today, Germany is made up of sixteen states called *Länder* (the plural form of *Land*). Three states – Berlin, Hamburg and Bremen – are also cities. The remaining thirteen states are Schleswig-Holstein and Lower Saxony (Niedersachsen) in the north; Mecklenburg-West Pomerania (Mecklenburg-Vorpommern), Thuringia (Thüringen), Brandenburg, Saxony-Anhalt (Sachsen-Anhalt) and Saxony (Sachsen) in the east; Saarland, Rhineland-Palatinate (Rheinland-Pfalz), North Rhine-Westphalia (Nordrhein-Westphalien) and Hesse in the west; and Baden-Württemberg and Bavaria (Bayern) in the south.

THE GERMAN LÄNDER

Germany consists of sixteen states, or *Länder*, including the city-states of Berlin, Bremen and Hamburg. The states are listed below with their capitals, which are marked on the map with a dot.

BADEN-WÜRTTEMBERG	NORTH RHINE-WESTPHALIA
Stuttgart	Düsseldorf
BAVARIA	RHINELAND-PALATINATE
Munich	Mainz
BERLIN	SAARLAND
Berlin	Saarbrücken
BRANDENBURG	SAXONY
Potsdam	Dresden
BREMEN	SAXONY-ANHALT
Bremen	Magdeburg
HAMBURG	SCHLESWIG-HOLSTEIN
Hamburg	Kiel
HESSE	THURINGIA
Wiesbaden	Erfurt
LOWER SAXONY	
Hanover	
MECKLENBURG-WEST POMERANIA	
Schwerin	

North Germany

Schleswig-Holstein, Germany's northern-most state, lies on the Jutland Peninsula between the North and Baltic seas. To the north lies Denmark. For many years, Schleswig-Holstein was under the control of Denmark, and today its culture has many Scandinavian influences. Inland, Schleswig-Holstein comprises forests, marshes and farmland, while the coastline is dotted with fishing villages and small trading ports. Islands off the Baltic coast – in particular Sylt, which is the sunniest place in Germany – teem with tourists in summer. The state capital is Kiel, a busy sea port.

To the south-west of Schleswig-Holstein lies Lower Saxony. Although it is one of Germany's larger states, Lower Saxony has only a small population. Its diverse landscape encompasses plains, low mountains, bleak heathland and the North Sea coast. Offshore lie the East Frisian and North Frisian island chains, both popular holiday destinations.

The Frisian Islands are the homelands of the Frisians, an ethnic group that has preserved its distinct language and culture. The Frisian language, which is also spoken in parts of the north German mainland, was the basis of much of Old English, the language that lies at the root of modern English. Frisian resorts and spas along the North Sea attract many health-conscious Germans. The state capital of Lower Saxony is the ancient city of Hanover. Many of its beautiful buildings were destroyed during World War Two (1939–45).

Heathland is a feature of the landscape of Lower Saxony. Much of the huge Lüneburg Heath lies here. The heath stretches from Hanover in the south of Lower Saxony north to the city-state of Hamburg.

Eastern Germany

Of the sixteen states that make up present-day Germany, five (including Berlin) lie in what was formerly East Germany. These states did not exist between 1952 and 1990, but were re-created when Germany was reunified.

The area made up by Mecklenburg-West Pomerania, Brandenburg, Saxony-Anhalt and Saxony was once part of East Germany, the **communist** state that existed between 1952 and 1990. In earlier times, much of this land was part of the mighty empire of Prussia that once stretched across a vast area of north-eastern Europe.

Mecklenburg-West Pomerania lies to the south-east of Schleswig-Holstein. Its countryside is dominated by its coastline and, inland, by ancient forests and lakes. The land remains much as it was hundreds of years ago, and the small population lives on farms and in scattered towns and coastal ports. The state also includes rugged Rügen, Germany's largest island, separated from the mainland by a narrow channel called the Strelasund. Mecklenburg-West Pomerania's capital is Schwerin, which was built beside a large lake.

South of Mecklenburg-West Pomerania, the sparsely populated state of Brandenburg encircles Berlin. Its countryside is mainly pine forest and farmland dotted with lakes and small towns. Special to this region is the Spreewald, a forested area inhabited by the Sorbs, a group that has lived in Germany for at least 1300 years (see box). The capital of Brandenburg is Potsdam, long the residence of the kings of Prussia.

Saxony-Anhalt is a diverse state. Its landscape includes heaths, marshes, plains and the thickly forested Harz Mountains. In the north, farmers cultivate Germany's richest soils. To the south is a large industrial region.

The Sorbs

The Sorbs are a Slavic people who have been settled within the territory covered by present-day Germany since about AD 631. Originally independent, they were engulfed by Germany's eastwards expansion in the Middle Ages.

Today, the Sorbs live in north-east Germany in the districts of Upper Lusatia in Saxony and Lower Lusatia in Brandenburg. They maintain their own language and culture, including the Sorb flag of blue, red and white horizontal stripes. The Sorbs are also called the Wends, a term that was once used to describe all Slavic peoples. The Wends left their mark throughout Germany. Berlin, Dresden and Leipzig among many others are Wendish place-names.

Medieval towns, cathedrals and monasteries abound throughout Saxony-Anhalt, and the state also boasts the small university town of Wittenburg, the birthplace of the **Protestant Reformation** of Martin Luther (1483–1546; see page 58). The state capital is Magdeburg.

Saxony is reputed to be the most politically conservative state in Germany, although citizens in the city of Leipzig spearheaded the peaceful protests that helped overthrow East Germany's communist government (see page 75). Much of the state is heavily polluted due to extensive mining of brown coal (lignite). Saxony's capital is Dresden. Once a centre of culture and the arts, the city was heavily bombed during World War Two.

Thuringia's main contribution to Germany is cultural. This rural state is dominated by its dense forest. In the past, the state's aristocrats built numerous palaces and castles there – more than are found anywhere else in the country. They also supported the arts, encouraging the growth of vibrant cultural centres, such as Weimar, the home of Germany's golden age of literature and the original seat of the Weimar Republic (see page 64). Under the former East German government, heavy industries prospered in the state but today they are mostly shut down. The capital is Erfurt.

Dresden is known around the world for the destruction it suffered from bombing during World War Two. Today, its citizens are still working to restore the city to its former beauty.

A Rhine legend

A long poem written in the early 13th century, the *Nibelungenlied* (*Song of the Nibelungs*) is a tale of magic, greed, treachery and revenge. It is set partly in the Rhine-Palatinate city of Worms, which was the capital of the duchy of Burgundy in the early Middle Ages. Central to the story is a hoard of gold that belongs to the Nibelungs, a wicked Burgundian family. This hoard passes first to Siegfried, a German knight and hero of the poem, then to Hagen, who kills Siegfried. Before he is himself killed, Hagen buries the treasure at a secret spot at the bottom of the Rhine, possibly near the Lorelei rock, where it remains undiscovered.

Western Germany

The west of Germany is dominated by the mighty Rhine and its tributary, the Ruhr. The state of North Rhine-Westphalia is heavily industrialized, especially in the mineral-rich Ruhr River valley. North Rhine-Westphalia holds the distinctions of having the highest population in Germany and the highest population density in Europe. The capital of the former West Germany, Bonn, is found here, along with many other urban centres. These have a multicultural flavour thanks to the large influx of immigrants since World War Two. The populations of these towns and cities include communities of Greek, Turkish, Serbo-Croat, Italian and Spanish peoples.

To the south is Rhineland-Palatinate. This is home to some of Germany's most popular legends, inspired by the state's many ruined castles and the Rhine River. The story of the *Nibelungenlied* (*Song of the Nibelungs*, see box) is set in this region, as is the tale of the Rhine's Lorelei, whose song lured sailors to their death on the river's rocks. The state has many industries, but it is also agricultural, with vineyards along the Rhine River valley. Cities include the state capital, Mainz, as well as Worms, Speyer and one of Germany's oldest centres, Trier, founded by the Romans some 2000 years ago.

Situated along the borders of Luxembourg and France, the Saarland has a French heritage. The region is named after the Saar River, a tributary of the Mosel. Until the early 1800s, the area belonged mainly to France; it then became a disputed region until Saarlanders voted to join West Germany in 1957. The French influence is still clear from the traditional Saarland greeting 'salü', which is similar to the French 'salut'.

Once a source of valuable minerals such as coal, the Saarland was highly industrialized in the past. Its resources now depleted, the state has the weakest economy in the country and suffers from high unemployment. Like many other German cities, the capital, Saarbrücken, was badly damaged in World War Two.

Roughly in the centre of Germany lies Hesse, a region of hilly farmland and dense forest with its capital at Wiesbaden. Hesse is also an important economic centre. Frankfurt is now Germany's banking and finance capital. Traditionally, it was the centre of the European book trade and still hosts an international book fair.

South Germany

The state of Baden-Württemberg enjoys a prosperous economy based on cutting-edge technological industries. It is also famous for its holiday spots, including the Black Forest and the Bodensee (Lake Constance). The best known of Germany's lakes, the Bodensee also shares borders with Switzerland and Austria.

Lindau sits on an island close to the German shore of the Bodensee and is connected to the mainland by bridges.

The fairy-tale castle of Neuschwanstein above the Pöllat River was built by Ludwig II of Bavaria (1845–86). The king was inspired by the legends of German chivalry and their interpretation by the composer Richard Wagner (1813–83).

The old town of Heidelberg is one of the most beautiful and romantic places in Germany. Cobblestoned streets lead up to an old castle, and the town below is busy with students who attend the town's prestigious university. The region of Baden-Württemberg also preserves many old monasteries, including Maulbronn, situated between Karlsruhe and the state capital, Stuttgart.

Bavaria, also in southern Germany, is the country's largest state and also one of its most distinct. The people are particularly proud of their culture and speak a version of German that is much softer than that spoken in the north. Bavaria has breathtaking mountain scenery that includes rolling hills and part of the Alps. The countryside of this wealthy, industry-rich state is dotted with farms, mountain villages, medieval towns and romantic castles. In the south is its elegant capital, Munich (München), home of the **Oktoberfest** beer festival.

The city-states

The cities of Berlin, Bremen and Hamburg held special status even before the unification of Germany in 1871. Hundreds of years ago, they established themselves as prosperous, powerful centres of trade, culture and learning. Today, they are still self-governing cities, not part of any of Germany's states. In addition, they continue to hold the status of states as well as cities.

CLIMATE

Germany has a temperate, or mild, continental climate, which means that extreme weather conditions are rare. Regional climates vary according to factors such as the nearness of the sea, altitude and winds.

In the north and north-west, the climate is generally very mild. Rain tends to fall evenly throughout the year because moist winds continually blow in from the sea. The temperatures of the North and Baltic seas, as well as the Atlantic Ocean, do not change much from season to season, and their waters moderate both cold winter winds and hot summer air. Further inland, to the south and east, winters are colder and summers are hotter. Here, rain tends to fall mostly in the summer. Growing seasons are shorter than in coastal areas and there are more frequent frosts. Summers in the Alps are the shortest in the country. In winter, the mountains are covered in deep snow.

Germany's climate is also influenced by the movement of weather patterns across Europe. Winds from the west usually bring wet, warm weather, whereas winds from the east bring drier, colder conditions. Wind patterns can greatly affect seasons from year to year and can change the weather on a daily basis. A mild, dry wind called the Föhn sometimes blows down from the Alps, bringing warm, clear weather. The Rhine Valley is the warmest part of the country.

Annual rainfall on the Brocken – at 1142 metres (3747 feet), the highest peak in the Harz Mountains – is 160 centimetres (63 inches).

The chart shows the rainfall and temperature of two of Germany's major cities. The country has a fairly uniform climate, with warm, mild summers and cool winters.

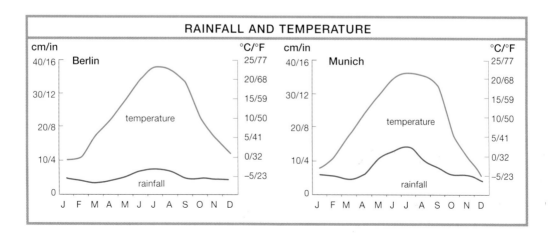

RAINFALL AND TEMPERATURE

WILDLIFE

Two species of martens can be found in Germany – the beech marten and the pine marten.

Despite Germany's heavy development and industrialization, a variety of animal species thrive. In the Alps live two species of wild goats – the Alpine ibex and the chamois. The Alpine ibex may be up to 1.5 metres (5 feet) long and stands up to 80 centimetres (32 inches) at the shoulder. It is brownish in colour, and the male has tall, knobbly horns that curve backwards towards their tips. The female's horns are much smaller. The chamois is a little smaller than the ibex and is light brown in summer with a dark stripe down the centre of its back. Its face is white with a black mask, and its short horns curve sharply at their tips to form hooks. In winter, the chamois has a shaggy, dark brown coat.

The Alps are also home to one of Germany's most magnificent birds, the golden eagle. At the opposite end of the country, the white-tailed eagle, a relative of the bald eagle, can be found on the lakes of the North German Plain, as can the osprey, a fishing bird of prey and summer visitor. Another summer migrant is the white stork, which nests on the roofs of houses.

Germany once had populations of brown bears and grey wolves. These species are now extinct in Germany in the wild, although wolves still exist in neighbouring countries to the east and cross into Germany from time to time. The lynx also sometimes occurs in the east of the country, while another cat, the wildcat, can be found in the Eifel, Hunsrück and Harz mountains and around the Elbe Valley. The wildcat looks much like a striped domestic cat but has a thicker, bushier tail. Other carnivorous (meat-eating) animals that inhabit parts of Germany's countryside include pine and beech martens, polecats, weasels and river otters.

The golden eagle is an inhabitant of Germany's southern mountain ranges.

Wild boar

The ancestor of the domestic pig, the wild boar measures up to 1.8 m (6 ft) long and stands up to 1 m (39 in) at the shoulder. Males have curly upper tusks and straight lower ones.

The wild boar lives in deciduous woodland and feeds mainly at night on bulbs, tubers and acorns. Mating takes place in winter, and up to ten brown-and-cream-striped young are born in spring or early summer.

Germany's populations of wild boars live in the forests of the south and east and are hunted as game animals.

Besides the ibex and the chamois, Germany's large herbivores (plant-eaters) include the wild boar and several species of deer, among them the fallow deer, the red deer and the elk, which strays in from the country's eastern neighbours. Among the smaller herbivores are the mountain hare, the brown hare and the beaver, which is similar to the North American species. In the Elbe Valley, the beaver was threatened with extinction, but today it and other threatened species, such as the eagle owl, are protected by strict wildlife laws.

Germany's amphibians and reptiles include salamanders, lizards and snakes, although only one species of snake – the adder – is venomous. The adder belongs to the viper family. It generally measures about 30 centimetres (12 inches) long and eats small mammals, other reptiles and small birds.

The European elk is the same species as the North American moose, whereas the North American elk is the same species as the European red deer.

Germany's forests

Germany's land looked very different before people adapted it for agriculture and industry. Much of the country was covered with thick forests of broad-leaved trees such as oak, birch, beech and hornbeam, and also conifer trees such as spruce, pine and dark and silver firs. Over many centuries, people cut down most of these trees for fuel or timber or to clear farmland.

Although about one-third of Germany today is covered by forests, less than half of these are original woodlands. The majority of wooded areas are made up of conifers planted in the 19th century, and many are planted as tree farms for forestry. However, these plantations do not possess the rich variety of wildlife and plants found in the country's natural woodlands.

Today, **acid rain** caused by air pollution is the largest threat to Germany's forests (see box opposite). To prevent a further reduction in the number of trees, strict laws are in place to attempt to reduce air pollution, and the logging industry is heavily regulated, too. More than half of Germany's forests are privately owned, but by law everyone is free to enjoy access to them for picnics, walks or bike rides.

In early 1990, it was reported that more than half the trees in East Germany had been damaged by air pollution.

National parks and nature reserves

Germans prize their wilderness and wildlife and manage them with great care. To protect unique natural areas from development, the government has created many nature reserves, where the number of visitors is closely controlled. One of the country's oldest and largest reserves is the Lüneburg Heath National Park, which was established in 1920 and covers 200 square kilometres (77 square miles) of Lüneburg Heath in northern Germany. The park's predominant plant is heather, the sweet smell of which attracts millions of bees. Many other kinds of plants, insects, birds and reptiles thrive in this national park, including the Heidschnucke, a breed of long-haired domestic sheep.

Like many breeds of domestic sheep, the Heidschnucke is descended from the mouflon, a wild sheep from the Mediterranean islands of Corsica and Sardinia.

Acid rain

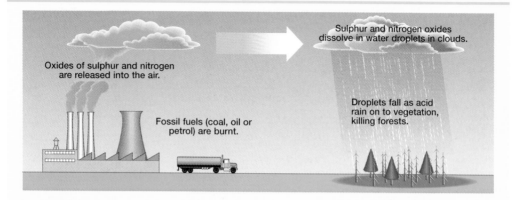

Oxides of sulphur and nitrogen are released into the air.

Fossil fuels (coal, oil or petrol) are burnt.

Sulphur and nitrogen oxides dissolve in water droplets in clouds.

Droplets fall as acid rain on to vegetation, killing forests.

Acid rain is produced when sulphur dioxide, nitrogen oxide and nitrogen dioxide are released into the atmosphere. There, these chemicals may turn into sulphuric and nitric acids, which dissolve in water droplets in clouds. The rain that falls from these clouds is highly acidic. It damages trees (as below), makes lakes unfit to sustain life and even eats away at buildings.

Scientists believe that a major cause of acid rain is the burning of fossil fuels. The former East Germany had high levels of air pollution largely because it burnt huge quantities of brown coal (lignite) to provide most of its electricity. Brown coal has a very high sulphur content. Since reunification, steps have been taken to change to less polluting fuels, such as oil and natural gas.

National parks

In addition to setting aside land for nature reserves, Germany also has twelve national parks to preserve areas of natural beauty.

SCHLESWIG-HOLSTEIN NATIONAL PARK

JASMUND

LOWER SAXONY WADDEN SEA NATIONAL PARK

VORPOMMERSCHE BODDENLANDSCHAFT

MÜRITZ

UNTERES ODERTAL

HIGH HARZ

HARZ   SÄCHSISCHE SCHWEIZ

BAVARIAN FOREST

BERCHTESGADEN

The city of Schwerin, founded in 1160, is the regional centre of the Mecklenburg Lake District and is built around no fewer than ten lakes.

In north-western Germany, the Lower Saxony National Park encompasses the islands of the coastal area, including the popular holiday destination of the East Frisian Islands. In the north-east is the Mecklenburg Lake District, one of Germany's last unspoiled areas of natural beauty. This region holds about 650 lakes, centred around the large Müritzsee (Lake Müritz) and Schweriner See (Lake Schwerin).

In the south-east of Germany is the Bavarian Forest National Park, which was set up in 1970 close to the border with what is now the Czech Republic. The park covers 130 square kilometres (50 square miles) of woodlands and high moors (*Filze*) and contains the peak of Grosser Rachel, which climbs to 1453 metres (4767 feet).

BERLIN: GERMANY'S CAPITAL

Located on the Spree and Havel rivers, Berlin is Germany's capital and largest city, with a population of about 3.5 million. The second-most important industrial centre in the country, Berlin is also one-third parkland.

History

The city began in the 1200s as a pair of settlements, Berlin and Kölln, which grew rich from trade and became united as the city of Berlin in 1307. Berlin continued to flourish. By the 19th century, it was one of the world's leading cities, famous for its palaces, parks and broad, busy streets. In 1871, Berlin became the capital of a unified German empire. During the following decades, the city grew into a major industrial centre, specializing in machinery, electrical goods and textiles.

The rulers of Brandenburg, the Hohenzollerns, made Berlin their capital in 1486. In 1701, the Hohenzollerns became the kings of Prussia.

In the foreground is Tauentzienstrasse, one of Berlin's main streets. In the distance is the Ku'damm.

The Nazi era

After surviving World War One (1914–18) unharmed, Berlin became one of the intellectual and artistic centres of Europe. It soon suffered economic crises, however, and became a battleground for extremist political parties, such as the **Nazis** and communists. After their rise to power in 1933, the Nazis purged Berlin of its diverse cultural and intellectual life.

During the restrictive Nazi years, an ambitious building programme was instigated by Germany's leader, Adolf Hitler (1889–1945). Hitler – himself a failed artist and would-be architect – aimed to make Berlin the world's most celebrated capital. Many of the structures were architecturally grandiose and most planned buildings were never completed. The Nazis plunged Germany into World War Two, during which some 50,000 buildings – more than 90 per cent of prewar Berlin – were devastated by bombing raids, shelling and street battles. Berlin's population fell to 2.8 million, compared with 4.4 million before the war.

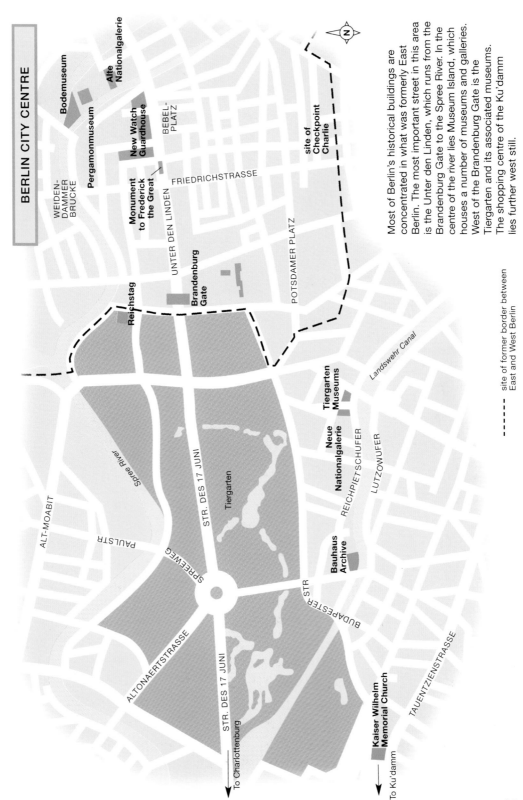

BERLIN CITY CENTRE

Most of Berlin's historical buildings are concentrated in what was formerly East Berlin. The most important street in this area is the Unter den Linden, which runs from the Brandenburg Gate to the Spree River. In the centre of the river lies Museum Island, which houses a number of museums and galleries. West of the Brandenburg Gate is the Tiergarten and its associated museums. The shopping centre of the Ku'damm lies further west still.

- - - - - site of former border between East and West Berlin

Bodemuseum

Alte Nationalgalerie

Pergamonmuseum

New Watch Guardhouse

WEIDEN-DAMMER BRÜCKE

BEBEL-PLATZ

site of Checkpoint Charlie

Monument to Frederick the Great

UNTER DEN LINDEN

FRIEDRICHSTRASSE

Reichstag

Brandenburg Gate

POTSDAMER PLATZ

Landswehr Canal

Tiergarten Museums

Neue Nationalgalerie

REICHPIETSCHUFER

LUTZOWUFER

Spree River

STR. DES 17 JUNI

Tiergarten

ALT-MOABIT

PAULSTR

SPREEWEG

Bauhaus Archive

BUDAPESTER STR

Kaiser Wilhelm Memorial Church

ALTONAERTSTRASSE

STR. DES 17 JUNI

To Charlottenburg

To Ku'damm

TAUENTZIENSTRASSE

35

East Berlin was the capital of East Germany from 1949 until the reunification of Germany in October 1990. During this period, West Berlin was a *Land* of West Germany.

A resident of the former East Berlin looks out from her apartment block.

Division and reunification

By 1949, Germany had been split into two countries – East and West Germany. Berlin lay in the middle of East Germany and was itself divided in two. West Berlin was rebuilt into a **democratic**, Western-style centre of business and industry, while East Berlin's recovery was restricted by strict communist control. In 1961, the government in East Berlin built the Berlin Wall to physically divide the two halves of the city. The much-hated wall was demolished in 1989, and in 1990 Berlin was officially reunited along with the rest of the country.

By the beginning of the 21st century, Berlin was thriving but also feeling the economic and social pangs of reuniting its affluent western half with the poorer eastern half. Districts in the western part of the city have changed little in recent years. The east is still filled with closed-down factories and shops, but many new businesses and vast construction projects are being built.

Modern Berlin

The site of the former wall is now a path marked with white crosses and plaques in memory of people from East Germany who were killed attempting to escape to West Germany. By the time Germany was reunified in October 1990, much of the wall had been torn down. A few small segments remain as memorials.

The Brandenburg Gate

The Brandenburg Gate was built in the late 18th century for King Frederick William II of Prussia (1744–97). It is the last survivor of Berlin's eighteen city gates. On top of the gate is a statue known as the Quadriga, featuring the Goddess of Peace driving a chariot. The original was destroyed in World War Two, and a copy using the old moulds was made in the 1950s. During the years of division, the Brandenburg Gate stood in no-man's-land between East and West Berlin.

Near the midpoint of this path stands the Brandenburg Gate, Berlin's most famous landmark (see box). This huge stone archway once represented the crossroads of Europe, and when Germany was divided after World War Two, it represented the dream of national unity. One of the capital's best-known streets, the Unter den Linden, begins at the Brandenburg Gate. The street's name means 'Beneath the Lime Trees'. Before World War Two, this elegant thoroughfare was lined with lime trees and was renowned for its cafés, restaurants and the performers and artists it attracted. The street lost its cultural life during the war, but since reunification, the Unter den Linden has been revitalized with new and expensive shops.

From the Brandenburg Gate, the Unter den Linden runs eastwards through the heart of eastern Berlin, where many of the finest monuments and buildings of past German empires still stand. Among these are a monument to King Frederick II ('the Great') of Prussia

In earlier times, the Unter den Linden was the route taken by nobles to go hunting in the woodlands that stood on the site of the Tiergarten.

The Siegessäule features the Goddess of Victory on top of a column some 60 metres (200 feet) high. It commemorates three successful military campaigns of the 1860s and 1870s. At one time located near the Reichstag, since 1938 the Siegessäule has stood in the centre of a huge traffic intersection on Strasse des 17 Juni in western Berlin.

(1744–97), a cultured ruler who doubled the size of the Prussian empire. Beyond, on the north side of the street, stands Humboldt University, originally built by Frederick as a palace for his brother. The university once employed the political thinker Karl Marx (1818–83), the scientist Albert Einstein (1879–1955) and the brothers Grimm, who compiled one of the world's most famous collections of fairy tales (see page 103).

A little further along on the left is the Neue Wache (literally, the New Watch; the building was originally a guardhouse), Germany's main memorial to victims of war and **totalitarianism**, and the Zeughaus German history museum. The Zeughaus, a former arsenal, was built at the turn of the 18th century and was the Unter den Linden's first large building. The Unter den Linden ends here, and a bridge crosses onto Museum Island. World-famous museums here include the Altes Museum, the Alte Nationalgalerie of 19th-century art and the Pergamon and Bode museums of early history. Near these museums is Oranienburgerstrasse – the heart of Berlin's old **Jewish** district. Revitalization of this area has included restoration of the New Synagogue, damaged by the Nazis in 1933 and by wartime bombs. Further east, the Alexanderplatz, which was once the seat of the communist government, is today filled with cafés and street performers.

Returning westwards in the direction of the Brandenburg Gate, the Unter den Linden passes by Bebelplatz, where in 1933 the Nazis burnt books written by forbidden authors. Further west, Friedrichstrasse crosses the Unter den Linden. Heading north, this street leads to the Weidendammerbrücke, and nearby stands the Theater am Schiffbauerdamm. This is the home of the Berliner Ensemble founded by the communist dramatist Bertolt

BERLIN UNDERGROUND RAILWAY

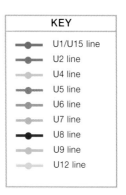

Afrikanische Strasse
Rehberge
Seestrasse
Amrumer Strasse
Westhafen
Birkenstrasse
Turmstrasse
Hansaplatz
Leopoldplatz
Wedding
Reinickendorfer Strasse
Zinnowitzer Strasse
Oranienburger Tor
Friedrichstrasse
Zoologischer Garten
Sophie-
Charlotte-
Platz
Uhlandstrasse
Wittenbergplatz
Potsdamer Platz
Mendelssohn-Bartholdy-Park
Kurfürstenstrasse
Kurfürsten-
damm
Nollendorfplatz
Augsburger
Spichemstrasse Str.
Strasse Güntzelstrasse
Hohenzollemplatz
Fehrbelliner
Platz
Heidelberger
Platz
Rüdesheimer Platz
Berliner
Strasse Innsbrucker Platz
Rathaus Schöneberg
Bayerischer Platz
Eisenacher Strasse
Kreistpark
Viktoria-
Luise-Platz
Bulowstrasse
Gleisdreieck
Möckernbrüke
Mohrenstrasse
Stadtmitte
Yorckstrasse
Mehringdamm
Paradestrasse
Tempelhof
Platz der
Luftbrücke
Gneisenaustrasse
Südstern
Boddinstrasse
Leinestrasse
Hermannstrasse
Franz-Neumann-Platz
Osler Strasse
Nauener Platz
Pankstrasse
Gesundbrunnen
Voltastrasse
Bernauer Strasse
Rosenthaler Platz
Schwartzkopffstrasse
Weinmeisterstrasse
Alexanderplatz
Klosterstrasse
Märkisches Museum
Französische
Strasse
Spittelmarkt
Hausvogteiplatz
Kochstrasse
Prinzenstrasse
Hallesches
Tor
Kottbusser
Tor
Görlitzer Bahnhof
Schönleinstrasse
Hermannplatz
Rathaus Neukölln
Karl-Marx-Strasse
Neukölln
Grenzallee
Blaschkoallee
Vinetasrasse
Schönhauser Allee
Eberswalder Strasse
Senefelderplatz
Rosa Luxemburg-Plaza
Schillingstrasse
Strausberger Platz
Jannowitzbrücke
Heinrich-Heine-Strasse
Mortzplatz
Warschauer
Strasse
Schlesisches Tor

KEY	
●—	U1/U15 line
●—	U2 line
●—	U4 line
●—	U5 line
●—	U6 line
●—	U7 line
●—	U8 line
●—	U9 line
●—	U12 line

Brecht (1898–1956). Heading south from the Unter den Linden, Friedrichstrasse arrives at Checkpoint Charlie. This was once the famous crossing point between East and West Berlin.

Beyond the Brandenburg Gate is what was formerly West Berlin. Close to the line of the Berlin Wall lies the Reichstag. Built in the 1890s, it housed the lower chamber of successive German parliaments until the 1930s. The building was burnt down in 1933, rebuilt, then damaged again during World War Two. Now that Berlin has been reinstated as the capital of Germany, the Reichstag building is once again home to the German parliament's lower house, now called the **Bundestag**. The Bundestag moved there from Bonn in 1999.

Close to the Reichstag and the Brandenburg Gate is the large park called the Tiergarten, which is about 4 kilometres (2½ miles) long and 800 metres (½ mile)

The new capital

The reunification of Germany in October 1990 paved the way for Berlin to once again become the capital of Germany. In 1991, the German parliament and government moved from Bonn to Berlin. New government offices, symbolic of the new Germany, were built around the old Reichstag building. The redevelopment of this area was seen as symbolic of the new political identity of the country after reunification. Offices of the government and the Federal Chancellery span the bend in the Spree River, symbolically joining the western and eastern parts of the city, thus ending old divisions.

The Reichstag itself has been converted by the British architect Sir Norman Foster. It houses the Bundestag in an environmentally friendly building. It has been designed so that it can be fuelled with vegetable oil, reducing carbon dioxide emissions by 94%.

Perhaps the most distinctive feature of the new building, however, is the glass dome at the top (see above). The dome, which occupies a central place on top of the old building, is open to the public and keeps new Germany's promise of a 'transparent parliament'. The renovated Reichstag was officially opened in May 1999.

wide. The park's main thoroughfare is the Strasse des 17 Juni (Street of 17 June). The name of the street commemorates the failed rising of East German workers against the communist authorities in 1953. The Tiergarten is filled with ponds, gardens, restaurants and museums, as well as the famous Berlin Zoo, which houses about 14,000 animals. Near the Tiergarten are the Bauhaus Archives

Potsdam

Potsdam lies on the Havel River 20 km (12 miles) south-west of central Berlin. Today, it is almost part of Berlin, but in the 17th century, when the Prussian court set up its summer quarters there, it was a quiet, rural retreat. Frederick II built palaces there, including Sanssouci. Later, German kings added buildings, among them Schloss (Castle) Cecilienhof. In July–August 1945, the Potsdam Conference on Germany's postwar future took place there.

and Museum. This collection is dedicated to the Bauhaus school of architecture and design, which was influential in the 1920s and early 1930s. Just up the street stands the Neue Nationalgalerie, which was built in the 1960s and houses a collection of modern art.

Beyond the Tiergarten, the heart of western Berlin lies along a boulevard named the Kurfürstendamm, or Ku'damm for short. Home to nightclubs and restaurants, the Ku'damm also boasts the city's finest hotels and shops. However, Berlin's largest department store is not on the Ku'damm but in nearby Tauentzienstrasse. Kaufhaus des Westens, or KaDeWe for short, is one of the largest stores in Europe.

Where Tauentzienstrasse meets the Ku'damm is the Breidscheidplatz, a square in which a monument to the destruction wrought by World War Two stands – the Kaiser Wilhelm Memorial Church. Dedicated to Wilhelm (William) I (1797–1888), the church was consecrated in the 1890s and all but flattened by bombs during World War Two. Only the church's broken bell tower remains as a memorial, looming eerily above the street, surrounded by the city's modern buildings. Among the most prominent of these is the Europa Centre, a 22-storey shopping and leisure complex constructed in the 1960s.

The old Prussian palace of Schloss Charlottenburg lies a good distance west of central Berlin. It was built between 1695 and 1790.

In 1963, US President John F. Kennedy delivered his 'Ich bin ein Berliner' ('I am a Berliner') speech at the Schöneberg town hall in Berlin to express solidarity with the people of West Berlin.

OTHER MAJOR CITIES

About 70 million Germans, or 86 per cent of the population, live in cities. Besides Berlin, the largest of these are Hamburg, Munich, Frankfurt and Cologne.

Hamburg is renowned for its docks, parks and churches and for the Inner and Outer Alster lakes, on which sailing and other watersports take place.

Hamburg

Hamburg is Germany's second-largest city and is known for its wealth, nightlife and business-like atmosphere. It is the country's largest port and is home to imposing steelworks and ironworks, shipyards and manufacturing plants. It is also the country's media centre and a hub of chemical and high-tech industries. Hamburg's extensive industry is balanced by a strict policy promoting greenery – half the city is beautiful parkland. A canal network criss-crosses the centre, and Hamburg has more bridges than Venice or Amsterdam.

Although most of its buildings did not survive the bombing raids of World War Two, Hamburg recovered quickly. A few ruins, such as the tower of St Nikolai Church, are left as war memorials in the old city centre. Not far away from these ruins is one of the more unusual sights of Hamburg – the Chilehaus, a 1920s office building in the shape of a huge ship. Also nearby stands

HAMBURG CITY CENTRE

the city's symbol and its most celebrated church, St Michael's. It has been rebuilt three times after being damaged by lightning, by fire and finally by bombing.

A flea market takes place weekly on the waterfront in the shadow of Hamburg docks.

Impressive sights in Hamburg include the Köhlbrandbrücke, a suspension bridge built in 1975 across an arm of the Elbe; the Alster, an artificial lake in the heart of the city; and the Hopfenmarkt, a large public square. Hamburg is famous for the Reeperbahn, a street of nightclubs, including the Star club where the Beatles played nightly in 1960.

The heart of Hamburg, however, is its huge sea port, lined with modern heavy equipment. Entering Hamburg by sea, a ship has to sail 80 kilometres (50 miles) up the Elbe estuary, which is lined with vast mansions and beautiful trees. As the vessel enters the port, the national anthems of Germany and the ship's country are played as a welcome on a loudspeaker located on the river.

The Elbe River is one of the world's busiest shipping routes. More than 13,000 vessels of all kinds pass along the river each year.

In the 16th century, Hamburg was a haven for Protestants and for Jewish refugees from Portugal. In the 19th century, the city was the main point of exit for millions of European religious and economic refugees bound for the USA. The composers Felix Mendelssohn (1809–47) and Johannes Brahms (1833–97) were both born in Hamburg.

MUNICH CITY CENTRE

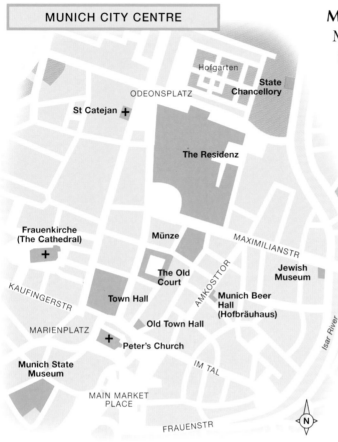

Hofgarten

ODEONSPLATZ

State Chancellory

St Catejan ✚

The Residenz

Frauenkirche
(The Cathedral)
✚

Münze

MAXIMILIANSTR

Jewish Museum

KAUFINGERSTR

The Old Court

AMKOSTTOR

Munich Beer Hall (Hofbräuhaus)

Town Hall

Old Town Hall

MARIENPLATZ

✚ Peter's Church

Munich State Museum

IM TAL

Isar River

MAIN MARKET PLACE

FRAUENSTR

N

Munich

Munich (called München in German) was once the capital of an independent Bavaria, during which time the grand buildings that now house many of the city's galleries and museums were constructed. Because of its stylish fashions and sunny, relaxed atmosphere, the city of Munich is sometimes called the 'German Paris'. Many people are drawn by the city's cultural life and its closeness to the Alps, as well as by the Oktoberfest (October Feast) beer festival. The city attracts designers, artists, writers and the wealthy, and is a centre of education for thousands of students. Electrical equipment and optical and precision instruments are made in Munich, and many international exhibitions and trade fairs are held there. Since the late 18th century, the city has been a major printing and publishing centre. There are also clothing manufacturers and textile factories.

Munich's main attractions include the Frauenkirche church and the Hofbräuhaus in the city centre. Local legend says that a footprint in the entrance of the Frauenkirche is that of the devil. The story goes that in order to complete the building, the church's architect made a pact with the devil in return for his soul, but later fooled the devil and kept his soul. The Hofbräuhaus,

Munich city centre lies on the west bank of the Isar River. Three of the old city gates still exist, all dating back to the 14th century. Isartor (Isar Gate) is to the east of the city, Sendlinger Tor (Sendlinger Gate) on the south side and Karlstor (Charles' Gate) on the west side.

called 'the most famous pub in the world', is a beer hall dating as far back as 1589. Inside, the spirit of Oktoberfest lives year-round as countless patrons crowd along wooden benches to drink beer. In the centre of Munich is the Residenz, a large 14th-century palace built by Bavaria's ruling noble family. This ornate building includes museums, fountains, artworks and a stunning theatre now used by the city for the performing arts.

After World War One, Munich was at the heart of the political upheavals that accompanied the rise of Nazism. In 1923, the Nazis staged an anti-government uprising there known as the Beer Hall Putsch (see page 65). In 1938, Hitler set his sights on taking over areas bordering Germany that were populated by ethnic Germans. Representatives of the major European countries signed the Munich Pact, ceding to Germany an area in Czechoslovakia known as the Sudetenland. Heavily bombed at the end of World War Two, Munich has been carefully and beautifully rebuilt and restored.

The Oktoberfest dates back to the wedding of Crown Prince Ludwig of Bavaria and Princess Therese in October 1810. A festival has taken place in Munich each October ever since.

The Residenz was begun in 1385 and was the main home of the Wittelsbach family, who ruled Bavaria from 1180 until 1918.

Frankfurt boasts 137 museums, twelve of which are situated on the banks of the Main River in the so-called Museumsufer. The city was closely connected with the election of the Holy Roman emperors – the old city hall is called the Römer (the German word for 'Romans').

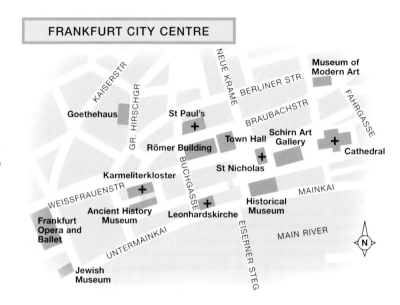

FRANKFURT CITY CENTRE

The Commerzbank is one of more than 400 banks that have offices in Frankfurt.

Frankfurt

Located on the Main River at the heart of Germany, Frankfurt is the country's financial centre and home to Germany's leading stock exchange and the country's central bank – the Bundesbank. The city hosts a number of international trade fairs, among them the huge Frankfurt Book Fair, which takes place each autumn. Frankfurt's modern, American-style skyline was built after most of the city's buildings were destroyed in World War Two.

Frankfurt has gained a world reputation for its museums, theatres and galleries. In fact, it spends more on the arts than any other city in Europe. Visitors are attracted to both the ancient sights in Frankfurt, such as the Römerberg – a low hill on which ancient forts and settlements are located – and the many modern buildings that house Frankfurt's cultural centres and galleries. The poet, dramatist and scientist Johann Wolfgang von Goethe (1749–1832) lived in Frankfurt, and the house in which he was born has now been converted into the Goethehaus museum.

Cologne

The fourth-largest city in Germany, Cologne (Köln in German) is also one of its oldest. Founded by the Romans, it rose to prominence during medieval times, when thousands of Christians made pilgrimages to its 150 churches. It also became well known in the 18th century for its invention – the fragrance known world-wide as *eau de cologne* (cologne water). The phrase has now come to mean simply 'perfume'.

Today, Cologne is a modern, lively centre of trade and business. Its **cathedral**, the most visited monument in Germany, dominates the city from the old town centre. Begun in 1248 and not completed until 1880, it is one of the largest Gothic buildings in the world. Close by are museums filled with ancient treasures and contemporary art. About 25 per cent of Cologne is dedicated to green spaces, and its most popular park is the Rheinpark along the Rhine River, which hosts garden shows and summer concerts.

The great Gothic cathedral of Cologne reputedly contains the remains of the Three Wise Men, who visited the baby Jesus Christ.

Ninety per cent of Cologne's centre was destroyed in 1945 at the end of World War Two. However, numerous ancient buildings survived or were rebuilt.

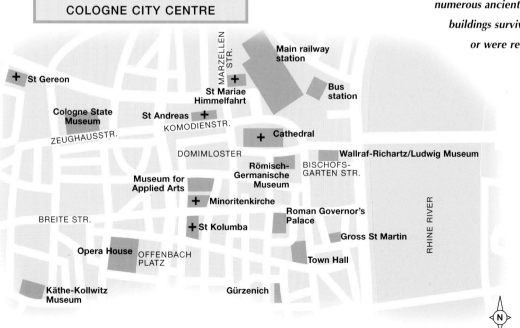

COLOGNE CITY CENTRE

St Gereon
Cologne State Museum
ZEUGHAUSSTR.
MARZELLEN STR.
Main railway station
St Mariae Himmelfahrt
Bus station
St Andreas
KOMODIENSTR.
Cathedral
DOMIMLOSTER
Wallraf-Richartz/Ludwig Museum
Römisch-Germanische Museum
BISCHOFS-GARTEN STR.
Museum for Applied Arts
Minoritenkirche
Roman Governor's Palace
BREITE STR.
St Kolumba
Gross St Martin
RHINE RIVER
Opera House
OFFENBACH PLATZ
Town Hall
Käthe-Kollwitz Museum
Gürzenich
N

Dü Lantgre
vin vō Düringe.

Lantgr: ine Hma
von Düringen.

hie krieget mit sange. h waltḥ vō d'vogilweide. h wolfrā von Eschubach
h Reimander alte. der tugenthafte schriber. heinrich vō ofterringē
vn klingesor von vngerlant.

Past and present

'This policy cannot be achieved through speeches ... it can be achieved only through blood and iron.'

19th-century German politician Otto von Bismarck

Although the nation of Germany did not exist until 1871, the history of the German people stretches back thousands of years, beyond the region's earliest written records. Today's ethnic Germans are descendants of tribes that had migrated to central Europe by about 100 BC. In the centuries since, the region has witnessed the rise and fall of empires, the building of great castles, **cathedrals** and canals, the birth of the **Protestant** religion and many devastating wars.

The early German tribes found themselves on the northern fringes of the western Roman empire, much of which they overran in the 5th century. The Germans eventually created another great empire in central Europe – the Holy Roman empire, which lasted from 962 until 1806. Presided over by a German king, it consisted of numerous territories, each with its own ruler. When the empire came to an end, the most powerful of the territories was Prussia. In 1871, Prussia united most of the other territories into the new country of Germany.

Germany's history in the 20th century was turbulent. The country suffered serious political and economic upheaval, largely because of its involvement in World War One (1914–18) and World War Two (1939–45). The latter, instigated by the **Nazi** leadership, led to the country being divided into **East** and **West Germany**. The two parts of Germany were reunited in 1990.

In medieval times, Germany's regional courts were important cultural centres.
The manuscript opposite shows poet-musicians from about 1305 to 1340.

FACT FILE

• The German leader Clovis I (466–511) became a **Roman Catholic** in the 5th century. Following his example, the Franks and many other German tribes also adopted **Christianity**.

• For centuries, the Holy Roman emperors were elected by German princes at Frankfurt and crowned in Rome by the pope. After the coronation of Maximilian II in 1562, however, they were elected and crowned at Frankfurt.

• The last German monarch was William II (1859–1941), who was emperor of Germany from 1888 to 1918.

This decorative wheel from a bed was found in southern Germany. It dates back to the 6th century BC.

PREHISTORIC GERMANY

Archaeologists estimate that the region of present-day Germany has been inhabited for up to 650,000 years. By studying fossils, pottery shards, bones and other remains, scientists have concluded that a succession of peoples has lived there. Many were nomads, but others settled and built villages and farms.

One of Germany's most remarkable prehistoric sites is at Bilzingsleben, near Magdeburg in north-eastern Germany, where archaeologists discovered evidence of early human activity. Judging by a human skull found there, this lakeside site is over 400,000 years old. Scientists believe that the people of Bilzingsleben lived by gathering nuts and berries and by hunting large animals, including rhinoceroses and elephants. They also killed beavers for their fur. Bones of predators such as wolves, bears and lions have also been found.

Between 130,000 and 35,000 years ago, Europe was inhabited by Neanderthals, a type of early human now extinct (see box). Scientists distinguish Neanderthals by their massive brow ridges and small, sloped foreheads. Their name comes from the place where their remains were first discovered – the Neander Valley (Neanderthal in German) in western Germany, east of Düsseldorf.

Neanderthals

Neanderthals were a subspecies of the species *Homo sapiens*, to which modern humans belong. Shorter and more heavily set than other early humans of the time, Neanderthals lived across Europe and the Middle East in a range of environments. Scientists believe that one reason for their physical differences from other early humans was that they were the first group to live in cold climates.

Neanderthals made tools and hunted animals such as mammoths and wild oxen. They gathered plant food when it was available. A Neanderthal's brain was similar in size to that of a modern human, and some scientists believe that Neanderthals were the first humans to bury their dead. It is unclear whether the Neanderthals became extinct or were absorbed into other early human groups.

CELTS, GERMANI AND ROMANS

The first permanent settlements in the German region were those of the Celts, who lived throughout central Europe by 400 BC. The Celts were excellent farmers and warriors as well as skilled metalworkers. The Celts left behind many examples of fine craftsmanship in iron, bronze, silver and gold. Since these and other early peoples of the region left no written history, most information about them comes from artefacts, such as tools and weapons, excavated from settlements and graves.

By 100 BC, however, the Celts were driven from the region by the nomadic tribes of northern Europe. These northern tribes soon encountered the powerful Roman empire expanding from the south. The Romans called the northern tribes the Germani, or German tribes, and named their territory Germania.

The Romans tried to conquer Germania, but in AD 9, after three of their legions were crushed, the Romans abandoned their invasion and fortified their border with a wall called the *limes* (Latin for 'frontier'). During the following centuries, the German tribes launched many skirmishes against the Romans, but they also began to trade goods and knowledge. Eventually, the Romans hired German warriors to serve in the Roman army. By the late 4th century, however, the Roman empire in western Europe was weakened. German tribes crossed the *limes* and seized control of Roman territory. In AD 476, the German king Odoacer deposed the emperor in Rome and brought an end to the Roman empire in the west.

Having retired to the Rhine River after the defeat of AD 9, the Romans later retook some of Germania, then erected the limes. *Construction of these fortifications began in AD 83 under the Emperor Domitian.*

GERMANIA AD 14–280

Mare Germanicum

ROMAN EMPIRE

GERMANIA

ROMAN EMPIRE

- Germania
- Roman empire
- autonomous

N

The Germani were one of the many tribes in northern Europe. Others included the Vandals, Franks, Visigoths, Ostrogoths and Cherusci.

The maps below show the Frankish kingdom from the time of Clovis I to Charlemagne's death in 814. Present-day Germany is outlined in red.

THE GERMAN EMPIRES

From the late 5th century to the late 1800s, control of central Europe alternated between powerful rulers who commanded vast empires and hundreds of nobles who ruled small, self-governing territories. In 486, the first powerful German leader, Clovis I (466–511), led his tribe, the Franks, to victory over the Romans in what is now France. The Franks also conquered other German tribes, adding much of present-day Germany to their empire.

Charlemagne

After Clovis I died, the Franks' empire weakened and broke into many smaller, competing territories. In the late 8th century, however, Charlemagne (Charles the Great, 742–814) became leader of the Franks. He reunited the German tribes through wars and political alliances, creating another huge

FRANKISH KINGDOM IN 493

FRANKISH KINGDOM IN 714

FRANKISH KINGDOM IN 814

Aachen

Aachen (Aix-la-Chapelle in French) is today a small city in western Germany, close to the border with Belgium. In the 8th century, it was the capital of Charlemagne's huge empire. Charlemagne declared Aachen the 'new Rome' and built a palace and chapel there (see right).

The chapel, known as the Palatine Chapel, was built towards the end of the 8th century. The building eventually became a cathedral, and Charlemagne was buried there under the west door. The Frankish historian Einhard (c. 770–840) wrote about the life of Charlemagne, describing the church in the following way: '… [Charlemagne] built at Aachen a most beautiful church, which he enriched with gold and silver and candlesticks, and also with lattices and doors of solid brass. When columns and marbles for the building could not be obtained elsewhere, he had them brought from Rome and Ravenna ….'

Over the next millennium, sections were added and many people contributed to the cathedral's treasures, which included the Four Great Aachen

Relics that attracted Christian pilgrims from all over Europe. The relics were believed to be the bones of the Three Wise Men, who visited Christ at his birth. From 936 to 1531, 30 German kings were crowned in the cathedral. The building was badly damaged during World War Two and parts of it have been rebuilt.

The lowercase (small) letters – a, b, c and so on – that we use today derive from those that Carolingian scribes used. They are called Carolingian minuscule. Previously, the Roman alphabet had only capital letters.

The Holy Roman empire in 1378 contained many territories that lie outside present-day Germany.

empire that spanned northern Europe. Wanting to revive the civilization of the Romans, Charlemagne established an organized government, set up schools and encouraged the arts. His reign is sometimes called the Carolingian **Renaissance** ('Carolingian' is the adjectival form of Charles). In 800, the pope crowned Charlemagne emperor of the Romans, a title meant to recall the glory and power of the leader of the ancient Roman empire.

The Holy Roman empire

Charlemagne entrusted much of his empire's defence to local leaders, granting them lands and noble status. After his death in 814, Charlemagne's empire broke into territories, each ruled by a local noble leader. In 919, the noble leaders east of the Rhine River elected a new ruler for central Europe – Henry I (876–936) of the Saxons. Henry I led a powerful alliance of territories, which his son, Otto I (the Great; 912–73), expanded.

In 962, Otto I defended Rome against an attack, and in return, the pope crowned him the first Holy Roman emperor. This title confirmed Otto I's alliance with the Roman Catholic Church. Like the title 'emperor of the Romans' granted to Charlemagne, it also recalled the power of the ancient Roman emperors. For more than 800 years, the title of 'Holy Roman emperor' was bestowed upon each leader of the alliance, which became known as the Holy Roman empire.

Under the leadership of strong emperors, such as Frederick I (1123–90), known as Frederick

MEDIEVAL GERMANY

Amsterdam
Hamburg
Berlin
Brussels Cologne
Mainz
Prague
HOLY ROMAN EMPIRE
FRANCE
Basel
Munich
Vienna

Holy Roman empire
autonomous regions

N

Barbarossa ('red beard', see box), and his son Henry VI (1165–97), the Holy Roman empire grew to encompass hundreds of small territories in central Europe. During the reign of weaker emperors, however, the empire fell into disarray because its members argued over land, taxes and the power of the Church. Many of these disagreements turned into civil wars.

In 1273, Rudolf I (1218–91) became the first member of the Habsburg family to be named Holy Roman emperor. Until then, the Habsburgs were only a minor noble family, but for centuries after, they commanded the empire's largest group of territories, including their main territory, Austria. Habsburg emperors ruled almost continuously from 1428 until 1806.

Each of the hundreds of territories within the Holy Roman empire had its own ruler, customs and laws. Rulers bore titles such as 'duke', 'baron', 'prince' or 'bishop'; had their own courts, castles and armies; and collected their own taxes. Their subjects, mostly peasants, led hard lives in small rural villages or on farms in the countryside. The noble leaders provided peasants with food and shelter in return for their hard work.

As trade increased and towns prospered throughout the 1100s and 1200s, many people moved from the countryside to work as artisans, traders or labourers. As the trading towns grew into rich, powerful cities, many broke ties with the noble leaders and created their own governments. Some formed leagues for protection and to promote trade with one another, creating

Frederick Barbarossa

Frederick I (1123–90), named Barbarossa (meaning 'red beard'), was crowned Holy Roman emperor in 1155. He asserted himself over the German princes but was defeated when he tried to subdue Italy by force. He changed to a policy of peace and won the Italians over.

The picture shows the emperor in Crusader dress. He went on the Third Crusade in 1189, but drowned before he reached the Holy Land. Legend has it that he sleeps in the Kyffhäuser mountains in central Germany and will return to lead Germany to greatness.

The reinvention of printing

For a long time, it was believed that the German inventor Johannes Gutenberg (c.1390–1468) was the first person to print a book using movable type – that is, with reusable wood or metal stamps. Gutenberg's Latin Bible, published in 1455, was the first book to be printed in Europe, but historians now know that printed books were being made hundreds of years before by the Chinese.

Historians debate about who first invented movable type. In about 1700 BC, the ancient inhabitants of Crete, called the Minoans, seem to have used reusable stamps to create symbols on a clay tablet known as the Phaistos Disc. Movable type made from earthenware was made in China in AD 1041, and metal type was invented in Korea in about 1300. Because written Korean and Chinese used thousands of pictographs instead of a relatively small alphabet, movable type was never popular in these countries.

In Europe, however, Gutenberg's reinvention of movable type revolutionized society. Texts such as the Bible previously existed only as expensive, hand-written books, and only a few privileged people – usually Church members – were able to read and interpret them. After Gutenberg, the new printing presses could produce books more cheaply and efficiently. Books could be read by many more people. New ideas as well as traditional learning spread much more quickly, and more people could read and interpret a book like the Bible for themselves. Above is the opening page of Martin Luther's German translation of the Bible. Its fairly widespread availability after 1534 not only enabled many more Germans to read the Bible, but also helped to standardize the German language.

their own armies, navies, commercial laws and courts. The most powerful network was the Hanseatic League, which included the important trading cities of Bremen, Hamburg, Lübeck and Cologne.

The Protestant Reformation

Even before the Holy Roman empire was formed, conflicts arose between nobles, royalty and the Roman Catholic Church. Many people thought that the Church had too much political power, owned too much land and was too wealthy. Some felt it was not faithfully following Christian teachings. These feelings intensified after the Holy Roman empire was formed.

In 1517, a German priest, Martin Luther (1483–1546), wrote a list of demands for reforming the Roman Catholic Church (see page 58). His protest caused a storm of controversy. Church officials rejected Luther's ideas, but many people – even some Roman Catholic clergy – supported Luther. The reform movement, called the **Reformation**, was too strong for the Church to stop.

The Hanseatic League got its name from 'hansa', an old term for a 'guild of traders'. The league controlled virtually all trade in northern Europe and linked it with Mediterranean trading empires such as Venice.

The Reformation in Europe

The Reformation spread rapidly from its origins in Germany. By 1570, Protestantism was established in many parts of Europe. At the time of the Reformation, the Holy Roman emperor was the Habsburg Charles V (1500–58), who was also king of Spain.

Martin Luther

The German preacher and scholar Martin Luther (1483–1546) was born in Eisleben, a town in Saxony. In 1507, after graduating from university, he became a priest of the Roman Catholic Church. Luther went on to teach theology – the study of God and religion – at a university in Wittenberg, also in Saxony, overlooking the Elbe River. There, his brilliant lectures on the Bible attracted scores of students. Starting in 1514, Luther also worked as a parish priest. He believed that the Bible ought to be made understandable to ordinary people. There was no German translation of the Bible, so it could be read only by priests and scholars who could read Latin, ancient Greek or ancient Hebrew. In his sermons, Luther tried to make the Bible relevant to the lives of his parishioners.

In 1510, Luther visited Rome and was shocked by the corruption of the pope and the Roman clergy. He was particularly angered by the Church's selling of indulgences to pay for the building of the lavish new church

of St Peter in Rome. Indulgences were church documents that excused a person's sins in return for the payment of money.

In 1517, Luther published his concerns about the Roman Catholic Church. Legend has it that he nailed his ideas, known as the *Ninety-Five Theses*, to the door of the castle church in Wittenberg. The new printing process (see page 56) allowed the theses to be published and read widely, and Luther's ideas were soon being fiercely debated across Europe.

At first, Luther had no intention of challenging the pope's supremacy. By 1519, however, he was in open revolt against the Roman Catholic Church. One of his ideas was 'justification by faith alone', by which a Christian gained salvation only by sincere and conscientious belief and not through the intervention of the Church. In 1521, the pope expelled Luther from the Roman Catholic Church. Nevertheless, Luther refused to go back on his statements, reportedly saying 'Here I stand, I cannot do otherwise'. He was forced into hiding. Meanwhile, his influence spread rapidly across northern and eastern Europe. His insistence on the prime importance of the Bible helped to fuel the rise of new Protestant churches.

This portrait of Luther was painted in 1528 by his friend Lucas Cranach the Elder, who also portrayed Luther's ideas in art.

In the 1520s, Luther and his followers, called Protestants, established their own church. By the 1550s, many German people had become Protestants, and the Reformation had swept across Europe. The Roman Catholic Church responded with the Counter-Reformation, winning back many followers in the south of the Holy Roman empire.

The Reformation caused decades of upheaval throughout German lands. While many Protestants sincerely believed in reforming the Roman Catholic Church, others joined the movement for reasons other than religion. Some peasants thought that changing faiths would free them from their servitude to the nobility. Many nobles used the Reformation as an opportunity to seize lands from the Church or to challenge the authority of the Catholic Holy Roman emperors.

Charles V gave up the throne in 1558. His Spanish, Dutch and Italian lands passed to his son Philip II of Spain (1527–98). The Holy Roman empire passed to Charles' brother, Ferdinand I (1503–64).

The Thirty Years' War (1618–48) began as a religious conflict and became a struggle for power in Europe.

The Thirty Years' War

Religious strife was deepened by the power struggles between the Catholic Holy Roman emperor and Protestant noble leaders, and eventually exploded in 1618 in a series of devastating conflicts known as the Thirty Years' War. Fighting involved peasants, nobles, the emperor and even other countries. The nobles attacked the emperor and one another out of greed or vengeance. The rulers of Denmark, Sweden and France invaded German lands to expand their kingdoms.

Battles destroyed hundreds of towns and killed thousands of people. The war finally ended in 1648, when the Peace of Westphalia was signed. The truce forced the Holy Roman empire to give up land to its neighbours and grant independence to its Protestant territories.

THE THIRTY YEARS' WAR

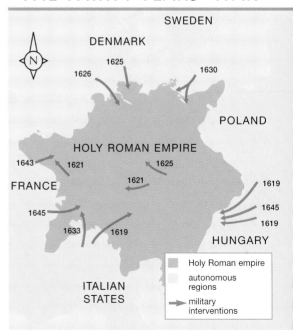

SWEDEN
DENMARK
N
1625
1626   1630
POLAND
HOLY ROMAN EMPIRE
1643 1621   1625
FRANCE   1621
1619
1645   1645
1633 1619   1619
HUNGARY

Holy Roman empire
autonomous regions
military interventions

ITALIAN STATES

Magdeburg in Saxony became a Protestant city during the Reformation and was besieged and burnt down by forces of the Holy Roman empire in 1630 and 1631. This etching of the destruction of the city was created in about 1718 for a German history book.

The growth of Prussia

The Peace of Westphalia strengthened the Holy Roman empire's largest Protestant territories. The most important of these was Prussia, which was ruled by a noble family called the Hohenzollerns. This ambitious family brought together Prussia and other territories by creating an efficient government and strong army, promoting the arts and constructing schools, roads and canals.

In 1756, the Hohenzollern king Frederick II (the Great, 1712–86) led Prussia's armies to war with Austria, which was the main territory of the Habsburgs and the Holy Roman empire. By the end of this conflict, called the Seven Years' War, Frederick II had defeated the Habsburgs and set Prussia on the road to becoming one of the most powerful nations in Europe.

The Napoleonic wars

Between 1789 and 1815, Europe was rocked by a series of uprisings and wars, beginning with the French Revolution and continuing during the rule of Napoleon

Bonaparte (1769–1821), who crowned himself emperor of the French in 1799. German territories, including Prussia and Austria, went to war to stop French expansion, but they were unprepared for Napoleon's armies.

In 1806, Napoleon defeated armies from Prussia and Austria, deposed the Habsburg family and put an end to the Holy Roman empire. He also claimed many German territories, including parts of Prussia, for his empire. Despite its losses, Prussia eventually rebuilt its armies and, together with Britain, finally crushed Napoleon at the Battle of Waterloo in 1815.

The last Holy Roman emperor was the Habsburg Francis II (1768–1835). After Napoleon's defeat of the empire, he continued to reign as Francis I of Austria until his death.

The German Confederation

After Napoleon's defeat, European leaders met at the Congress of Vienna (1814–15) to redraw Europe's borders and re-establish order. In recognition of Prussia's contribution, the congress awarded the Hohenzollerns a larger tract of land than they controlled before the wars.

The congress also created a new alliance of 39 German-speaking territories, including Prussia, called the German Confederation. The new confederation was not a success, however, because each territory kept its own ruler, laws and armies. States such as Prussia attempted to increase their own power at the expense of other members.

During the 19th century, the population of the German territories grew quickly as cities became **industrialized**. Millions of people moved from the countryside to the cities, looking for jobs in factories. Grinding poverty, a lack of **democracy** and a desire for a united German nation led to a revolution in the spring of 1848, but the confederation survived.

The 1848 revolutions

In 1848, unrest spread in a series of uprisings throughout France, Italy, the German territories and elsewhere. In each country, they were led by the middle class and nobility, who demanded a more democratic government and national self-rule. At the same time, workers and peasants protested against the poverty that had resulted from rapid industrialization. A time of discontent, 1848 also saw the publication of the *Communist Manifesto* by Karl Marx (see page 106) and Friedrich Engels.

In 1871, Prussia and the other German states (except Austria-Hungary) united to form Germany. The country also included Schleswig and Holstein, won from Denmark in 1865, and, in May 1871, Alsace-Lorraine, formerly part of France.

A UNITED GERMANY

In 1862, the king of Prussia, William I (1797–1888), appointed Otto von Bismarck (1815–98) to lead his government. Bismarck was a clever and ambitious politician who seized upon a growing feeling of **nationalism** among the German people as a means to build Prussia's power. He quickly led Prussia into three short, victorious wars against Denmark, Austria and France, dissolved the German Confederation and captured more land for Prussia. Other German states agreed to unite under Bismarck and William to form the new country of Germany, an event called German unification.

On 18 January 1871, William I was crowned kaiser (emperor) of Germany. Bismarck was appointed imperial chancellor (head of the German government). He worked relentlessly to strengthen the new country, bringing more than twenty German states into the union and overseeing the creation of colonies in Africa and the Pacific. He also forged a military partnership, the Triple Alliance, with Italy and Austria-Hungary.

Bismarck was called the Iron Chancellor because of his strong will and belief that political matters would be settled ultimately by 'blood and iron'. Throughout this nation-building period, Germany was transformed, as its government promoted rapid industrialization, military strength, scientific achievement and social welfare systems, such as subsidized housing. The people of Germany still lacked a strong voice in their government, however.

GERMANY IN 1871

German states

Prussia

newly acquired territories

autonomous nations

- - - boundary of German empire

- - - country borders

62

Bismarck's rule as chancellor came to an abrupt end in 1890, when he was dismissed by the new kaiser, William II (1859–1941). The new kaiser had his own, more aggressive plan to build up Germany's army and navy and broaden the nation's power worldwide. Britain, France and Russia soon formed a military partnership, the Triple Entente, to counter Germany's growing militarism and the threat posed by the Triple Alliance. As each partnership piled up weapons, Europe grew tense in anticipation of a great war.

Otto von Bismarck

The Bismarcks were an old family that lived in Brandenburg, then in Prussia. They belonged to the 'Junker' class, a powerful group of aristocratic Prussian landowners. Born on the family estate at Schönhausen in 1815, Otto von Bismarck entered the Prussian parliament in 1847 after studying law and agriculture. From 1851 to 1859, he was Prussia's representative at the German Confederation's assembly, before becoming Prussia's ambassador to St Petersburg, Russia, and then to Paris, France.

In 1866, Bismarck, now chief minister of Prussia, was made a count. At the end of the Franco-Prussian War five years later, he was made a prince. When his chancellorship ended in 1890, Bismarck was created Duke of Lauenburg and retired from public life.

War in Europe

Tensions ignited in the summer of 1914, after Archduke Ferdinand of Austria-Hungary was assassinated by a Serb at Sarajevo in Bosnia. An all-out war between the Triple Alliance and Triple Entente quickly broke out. Germany and its allies scored many victories at first, but their invasion of France was halted before they could capture the capital, Paris. Four years of bloody fighting followed, during which time Italy switched sides, Russia withdrew because of the revolutions of 1917 and the USA joined the side of the Entente.

By 1918, Germany's supplies were low, its armies exhausted and its citizens were protesting in the streets. Kaiser William II was forced to step down and allow a temporary government to take his place. On 11 November 1918, Germany surrendered. In retaliation for the war, Britain, France and the USA made Germany sign the Treaty of Versailles (see box page 64).

On 28 July 1914, Austria-Hungary declared war on Serbia, causing Russia to mobilize its armies. Germany declared war on Russia on 1 August, and two days later declared war on France and invaded Belgium. World War One had begun.

The Treaty of Versailles

The Treaty of Versailles agreed in Paris in 1919 stripped Germany of its colonies and parts of its land in Europe. North Schleswig (1) passed to Denmark, Eupen-Malmédy (2) passed to Belgium, Alsace-Lorraine (3) was returned to France, lands in the south-east of Germany (4) passed to Czecho-slovakia, lands in the east (5) passed to Poland and Memel (6) passed to Lithuania. The Allies occupied the rich industrial area of the Rhine Valley in western Germany and took resources such as coal. The city of Danzig came under the League of Nations. The agreement also severely limited the size and make-up of the German military, and demanded that large amounts of money and resources – known as reparations – be paid to the victors.

The Weimar Republic

The Spartacists took their name from the rebel gladiator Spartacus of ancient Rome. They opposed the German role in World War One and were later crushed by the military as a result.

In 1919, German politicians met in the city of Weimar to create a new, democratic government for their country. They established the office of president and an elected parliament. Supporters of the Weimar **Republic** hoped that it would become the most successful democracy in the world. From the beginning, the republic was opposed by parts of the army and by revolutionary **socialists**. Both groups tried to overthrow the government. In 1919, a **communist** group known as the Spartacists (see panel left) carried out a revolt. The army helped the government to put down the uprising. Soon after, two of its leaders, Karl Liebknecht (1871–1919) and Rosa Luxemburg (1870–1919), were found murdered.

In 1923, the extremist Nazis, led by Adolf Hitler (1889–1945), tried to overthrow the government in an event called the Beer Hall Putsch (revolt). It failed and its leaders, including Hitler, were jailed.

The republic was also hampered by severe economic problems, made worse by the huge reparations the country had to pay. Foreign help came in 1924 in the form of loans and reduced reparations. The German chancellor, Gustav Stresemann (1878–1929), reorganized the country's money and encouraged the growth of industry. For five years, Germany enjoyed relative peace and prosperity. In 1926, it joined the League of Nations.

Nevertheless, throughout the 1920s, high inflation (increases in prices), unemployment and shortages of food and goods were common throughout Germany. Germany's money plummeted in value, becoming almost worthless. At one stage in November 1923, one pound sterling was worth 2.6 billion German marks. Most people blamed these troubles on the enormous war reparations paid under the Treaty of Versailles. The hardships faced by Germans worsened after the US stock market crash of October 1929 plunged the world into economic depression. Germany suffered further severe economic problems and political troubles.

Many Germans lost faith in the ability of moderate, democratic politicians to find solutions to their country's problems. Throughout the 1920s, extremist political parties sprang up, their growth fuelled by the frustrations of people from all classes, but particularly people like small shopkeepers or office workers. The two strongest parties – the communists and the National Socialists (or Nazis) – campaigned hard and staged countless protests, many of which became violent street battles.

> The League of Nations was formed in 1920 and was the forerunner of today's United Nations Organization.

A 1919 poster for Germany's left-wing Social Democratic Party (SPD) demands 'Workers, open your eyes! Choose the SPD'.

THE NAZIS

Historians have sought to explain the rise of the National Socialists (Nazis) by pointing to currents of thought that existed in Germany in the decades before the 1920s. To an extent, Nazism grew out of 19th-century German nationalism. Nationalism is a strong form of patriotism that often includes a belief in one nation's superiority over others.

Hitler outlined his ideas in his book, *Mein Kampf* (*My Struggle*), which he wrote while in prison after the Beer Hall Putsch of 1923. Hitler believed that the Germans were superior to other nations. He dreamt of a great German empire that would not only unite all the German peoples of Europe but also spread deep into eastern Europe. The German race, he believed, had a sacred duty to create a powerful, authoritarian state that would rule other, 'lesser' peoples. Hitler hated democracy and, above all, he hated Jews and blamed them for all Germany's ills. Hatred of Jews is called anti-Semitism, and its origins can be traced back to medieval times when Jewish communities suffered segregation and massacres and were blamed for national disasters. In the 19th and early 20th centuries, anti-Semitic ideas existed in many parts of Europe and America.

During the 1920s and 1930s, the Nazis staged stirring mass rallies and marches and used clever publicity to

Hilter moulded the Nazi Party around his own obsessions, giving it a strongly militaristic character.

appeal to people's fears and insecurities. They recruited thousands of disillusioned officials and civil servants, bankrupt shopkeepers and small-business owners, and impoverished farmers and workers. Party members of 'pure' German blood willingly swore allegiance to Hitler. At its peak, the party had an estimated membership of about 7 million.

The Nazis often used violence in their struggle. The *Sturmabteilungen* (SA), or 'brownshirts', led by Ernst Röhm (1887–1934), were Nazi troops who beat up or murdered opponents, such as the socialists, and 'enemies', such as the Jews. Even more notorious were the elite, black-uniformed *Schutzstaffeln* (SS). The SS were commanded by Heinrich Himmler (1900–45), and after the Nazis came to power, they replaced the SA in 1934, effectively becoming Hitler's secret police.

The eagle was one of the symbols of Nazi Germany and took a number of forms. This version, with wings spread, sits perched on a swastika, the main Nazi emblem.

The Nazis come to power

The Nazis' first electoral success came in 1930, when they became Germany's second-largest party. As political turmoil increased, the aged president, Paul von Hindenburg (1847–1934), began to rule by decree; that is, without consulting parliament. Hindenburg's misuse of the emergency powers undermined democracy, so that people no longer believed that the republic worked. Two further elections in 1932 were inconclusive, although the Nazis became the largest party. In 1933, after an election in which the Nazis won many seats in parliament, Hindenburg appointed Hitler as chancellor.

Hitler quickly began to assume absolute control. After Hindenburg died in 1934, he changed his title to *Führer* (leader), adding the president's powers to his own. In just a few years, Hitler drastically reformed the government and the daily lives of Germans. He banned

The extreme nationalism of the Nazis is often called fascism. The term originated in Italy, where Benito Mussolini's Fascist Party came to power in 1922.

The Holocaust

The crimes of the Nazis are among the most notorious in history. Many of the Nazis' actions were based on their racist belief that Caucasian people of non-Jewish descent (Aryans), in particular of the Germanic type, were superior to other human beings. During their rule, the Nazis arrested as many 'inferior' peoples as possible, including Jews, Gypsies and Slavs under Nazi occupation. They also targeted political opponents, such as communists, and minorities such as homosexuals, together with many artists and intellectuals.

The picture below shows Nazis posting a notice on a Jewish-owned store in 1933. The poster reads: 'Germans, protect yourselves! Don't buy from Jews!' In 1935, the Nazis passed the Nuremberg Laws, which, among other restrictions, forbade marriages between Jews and non-Jews. To add to their humiliations, Jewish people were shut up in ghettoes – sectors of cities set aside for Jews only. Nazi victims were made scapegoats for Germany's problems and persecuted. Target groups were stripped of their rights, citizenship, jobs and property. Towards

the end of the 1930s, many millions of Nazi victims were forced to work as slaves in factories. Millions of others, such as the Gypsies in the picture above, were transported to concentration camps. There, some camp prisoners were used by Nazi scientists for horrifying medical experiments.

Then, in 1941 and 1942, the Nazis began what Hitler called 'the final solution of the Jewish question'. This was the deliberate extermination of the Jewish people – in Hebrew called *Shoah* (the **Holocaust**). Thousands of Jews were rounded up and shot by death squads after Germany invaded Russia. Of these, between 10,000 and 30,000 were killed in one two-day operation at Babi Yar, near Kiev, in September 1941. Jews in Germany and Nazi-occupied areas were rounded up and deported by train to death camps. There, they were gassed and cremated by the millions. By the end of World War Two, the Nazis had murdered some 6 million Jews and about 5 million Gypsies, Poles and other peoples.

The location of the principal Nazi death and concentration camps are plotted on the map of modern Europe below.

KOMM ZU UNS!

DEUTSCHES JUNGVOLK IN DER HITLER-JUGEND

This Hitler Youth poster calls on young Germans to 'Come to us!'

other political parties and took control of the courts, police, schools, newspapers and radio stations. This process was known as *Gleichschaltung*, which translates approximately as 'harmonization'. Everyone was expected to contribute to the regime. Boys of fourteen to seventeen years of age were encouraged to join the *Hitler Jugend* (Hitler Youth). There, they followed a rigorous programme of physical exercise and were indoctrinated with Nazi ideas. Girls joined the *Bund der Deutschen Mädchen* (League of German Girls).

The Nazis still terrorized and persecuted their opponents with beatings, imprisonment and murder. Some Germans approved of Hitler's policies. Others opposed some of his actions, but many supported his attempt to rebuild the country. Some Germans did not know about the Nazis' brutal tactics until it was too late to stop them. It is hard to know with certainty how many people truly supported or opposed Hitler, since those who spoke out against him were silenced.

Hitler envisioned building a German empire to rival the great empires of history. Ignoring the Versailles Treaty, he began rapidly rebuilding Germany's military forces. He also fuelled the public's resentment of the treaty to gain support for his actions.

At first, Hitler aimed to take over countries with substantial populations of ethnic Germans. In 1936, German forces re-entered the industrial zone of the

Pastor Niemöller

Martin Niemöller (1892–1984) was a Lutheran pastor. Born at Lippstadt, Westphalia, he was a submarine commander in World War One. After the war, he studied theology. He voted for the Nazis in 1924 but later realized that a free church could not exist in a Nazi state. He preached against Hitler and was arrested in 1937. He was kept first at Sachsenhausen concentration camp near Berlin and in 1941 was moved to Dachau, where he remained until 1945. After the war, he spoke out against German rearmament and the nuclear arms race and tried to improve relations with eastern Europe. In 1961, he became president of the World Council of Churches.

70

Rhineland. In March 1938, he proclaimed *Anschluss* (union) with Austria, and in September, under the Munich Agreement, he gained the German-speaking territory of the Sudetenland in what was then Czechoslovakia. Then, in March 1939, Hitler invaded the rest of Czechoslovakia and in August signed a pact with Russia – at the time, led by communists and called the Soviet Union (USSR) – agreeing to invade and divide Poland.

Nuremberg in Bavaria, an important centre of Nazism, was the scene of the Nuremberg Rallies, parades in which thousands of Nazi Party members participated.

WORLD WAR TWO

France and Britain feared the growing aggression of the Nazis and responded to Germany's invasion of Poland in September 1939 with declarations of war. Europe was not prepared, however, for the power and speed of the

German forces. Germany had built up a modernized air force – the *Luftwaffe* – and its army, spearheaded by tanks, attacked with a speed and efficiency that was previously unknown. The German mode of attack became known as *Blitzkrieg* (lightning war).

After quickly defeating Poland, Germany went on to capture Denmark, Norway, the Netherlands, Luxembourg, Belgium and, by June 1940, much of France. On 10 June, shortly before the fall of Paris, Italy became the second major Axis power to enter the war. During

German cities were pounded from the air throughout World War Two in an attempt to break national morale. Hamburg, pictured here in 1945, was subjected to 187 bombing raids during the conflict. One such attack, in August 1943, killed 45,000 people.

the summer and autumn of 1940, many air battles took place over Britain between Germany's *Luftwaffe* and Britain's Royal Air Force. However, with Britain committed to fighting on, Hitler switched his attention southwards and conquered the Balkans, Greece, Crete and parts of North Africa. Hitler had signed a non-aggression pact with the Soviet Union, but in June 1941, he betrayed his allies by sending an invasion force deep into Soviet territory. The invasion of the Soviet Union did not succeed as Hitler hoped, however, and it quickly joined Britain in fighting Germany. In December 1941, Japan, the third major Axis power, bombed the US naval base at Pearl Harbor in Hawaii. The USA immediately declared war on Japan, whose Axis partners, Germany and Italy, in turn declared war on the USA. The Axis of Germany, Italy and Japan was now confronted by the **Allies** led by Britain, the Soviet Union and the USA.

Through several years of bloody fighting, the Allies gradually took back lands seized by the Axis powers, all the while mounting devastating air attacks on German cities and industries. By April 1945, Allied troops were pushing into the German heartland. As the Soviets marched towards Berlin, Hitler committed suicide in his bunker. Germany lay in ruins, and its leaders surrendered days later.

Hitler called his regime the Third Reich ('Reich' is German for 'empire'). The first Reich was the Holy Roman empire and the second was Bismarck's Germany.

GERMANY DIVIDED

At the end of World War Two, troops from Britain, the USA, France and the Soviet Union occupied Germany. Each country controlled a portion of Germany. Its capital, Berlin, was also divided into four zones. The Allies

EUROPE AFTER WORLD WAR TWO

After its surrender in 1945, Germany lost territory in the east to Poland and the Soviet Union. The remainder of Germany was divided into zones supervised in the west by Britain, France and the USA, and in the east by the Soviet Union. Berlin was divided in a similar fashion.

met several times to decide how to rebuild the country. The Soviet Union, however, which was setting up communist governments in eastern Europe, disagreed with plans to establish a German democracy. By 1949, the Soviets had set up a communist government to rule their zone, calling the territory the Democratic Republic of Germany, or East Germany. Its capital was the Soviet-controlled zone of Berlin – East Berlin. The Soviet Union helped East Germany rebuild its cities and forge economic links with other communist countries. The East German government took control of all businesses, including banks, industries and farms, and controlled all production, wages and prices.

The same year, Britain, the USA and France combined their zones of occupation and helped Germans in these areas form a democratic country called the Federal Republic of Germany, or West Germany. Its parliamentary government was based in Bonn. Under the US **Marshall Plan** (see panel left), West Germany's recovery was based on **capitalism** and aided by the Western democracies.

The cold war

In 1955, West Germany entered the North Atlantic Treaty Organization (NATO), a military alliance formed in 1949 by the Western democracies. A year later, East Germany joined a similar Soviet alliance called the Warsaw Pact. Both alliances sent thousands of troops and deadly weapons to the two Germanys in preparation for a possible war. Despite their desire to be united, East and West Germans found themselves on opposing sides of this stand-off, called the cold war.

As years passed, it became clear that West Germany's recovery was much stronger than that of the East. West Germans enjoyed more freedoms and a higher standard of living. Thousands of East Germans fled to the West, mainly through Berlin, to escape the communist government's controls and to share in West Germany's wealth. In 1961, the East German government moved to

---

The city-state of Bremen in northern Germany lay in the British zone after World War Two. It was transferred to the US zone, however, to provide the USA with a port in occupied Germany.

Named after US secretary of state George Marshall, the Marshall Plan was an economic recovery programme.

From June 1948 to May 1949, the Soviets blockaded West Berlin after the Western Allies introduced a new German currency. During this time, the city was supplied by air (the Berlin Airlift).

THE COLD WAR

- Soviet bloc
- Western bloc
- neutral

ICELAND
FINLAND
NORWAY
SWEDEN
IRELAND
DENMARK
SOVIET UNION
UNITED KINGDOM
NETHER-LANDS
EAST GERMANY
POLAND
BELGIUM
WEST GERMANY
LUXEMBOURG
CZECHO-SLOVAKIA
FRANCE
AUSTRIA
HUNGARY
SWITZERLAND
ROMANIA
YUGOSLAVIA
PORTUGAL
SPAIN
ITALY
BULGARIA
ALBANIA
GREECE

In the era of East–West mistrust that followed World War Two, opposing alliances formed in Europe, with Germany sitting at their centre. The Western bloc was allied with the USA, while in the east a bloc formed that was allied with the Soviet Union. A handful of countries, such as the Republic of Ireland, remained neutral.

stop these escapes by cutting off east–west traffic across the border and building a wall through the centre of Berlin. East German guards were given orders to arrest or shoot anyone trying to escape over the Berlin Wall. Nevertheless, East Germans continued to attempt to cross the wall or the border into West Germany. Some were successful, but many died trying to flee.

In the decades after World War Two, people in both East and West Germany dreamt of reuniting the country, but this idea seemed impossible to achieve. Then, in 1989, the Soviet Union began to loosen its strict control over communist countries in Europe. In East Germany, hundreds of thousands of people began regular protests for greater freedoms and democratic elections.

In November 1989, the East German government finally agreed to let its citizens travel freely to the West. It also allowed non-communist political parties to form and announced the first democratic elections.

West Berlin was a West German 'island' isolated in East Germany. The East Germans strictly controlled access to the city from West Germany. Travellers by road could cross the East–West German border at four points; rail travellers at five. Three approved air routes also existed.

The Berlin Wall

The Berlin Wall stood for 28 years. When completed, it was 107 km (67 miles) long and an average of 4 m (13 ft) high. In East Berlin, there were guard towers with machine guns and other weapons. The East German government tore up the streets next to the wall, creating a no-man's-land of concrete, barbed wire, bunkers and trenches. The wall was under constant watch, with patrols of armed police with guard dogs. Of the few official crossing points, the most famous was Checkpoint Charlie, near the Brandenburg Gate. The wall separated friends, families, a city and a nation. In the picture, a West Berlin couple hold their twins above the wall so the children's grandparents in the East can see them.

Over the years, some 5000 people tried to escape into West Berlin. More than 100 died in the attempt, most being shot by East German border guards. Some people escaped through tunnels. The first successful tunnel was dug from an East Berlin graveyard. Mourners brought flowers to a grave and then dropped into the tunnel out of sight. A woman with a baby found the tunnel by accident and escaped, leaving the baby's pram. The police found the pram and closed the tunnel. Some escape routes were even more daring. In 1979, two East Berlin families secretly built themselves a hot-air balloon. After 23 minutes in the air, they landed on West German soil.

In 1989, the East German government finally allowed East Berliners to travel to West Berlin again. People flooded through the checkpoints. Some people began to break down the wall, and parties took place along its length. After reunification, the wall was taken down except for a few sections that remain as memorials to the once-divided city.

Most Germans were ecstatic about these sweeping reforms. In March 1990, East Germany's communist government lost the election, and more than 40 years of communist control came to an end.

REUNIFICATION

East Germany's new government was elected partly because it promised to reunite East and West Germany. A majority of West Germans also favoured this idea, and in August 1990, the two countries agreed on a treaty for reunification. On 3 October 1990, East and West Germany were officially reunited under the name of the Federal Republic of Germany. The event inspired enormous celebrations throughout the unified country.

Germans soon undertook the huge reforms needed to bring together the economies and social structures of the two former countries. These reforms proved extremely difficult, however, especially in what was the former

In January 1991, Helmut Kohl (born 1930), West German chancellor since 1982, was elected the first chancellor of the reunified Germany. He remained in office until 1998.

Willy Brandt

Born Herbert Ernst Karl Frahm in Lübeck, Willy Brandt (1913–92) became a socialist at the age of sixteen. As a journalist and opponent of the Nazis, he fled to Norway to escape arrest and changed his name. On his return home after World War Two, he was elected as a Social Democrat to the first parliament of the newly constituted Federal Republic of Germany (West Germany) in 1949.

Brandt first became known as a world figure as mayor of West Berlin from 1957 to 1966. By 1961, he had become the Social Democratic Party's candidate for chancellor and was eventually elected in 1969. He remained chancellor until he resigned in 1974 because of a scandal concerning an East German agent who had infiltrated his party.

Brandt's policy, called *Ostpolitik* (east politics), led in 1970 to the signing of non-aggression pacts between West Germany and the Soviet Union and Poland. He helped to bring about a free flow of traffic between East and West Berlin by 1971. The Brandt administration brought West Germany into full participation in the world community. Brandt was awarded the 1971 Nobel Peace Prize for his efforts towards easing tensions between eastern and western Europe.

East and West Berliners meet on the Berlin Wall near the Brandenburg Gate on the night of 9 November 1989. This was the night the wall, since 1961 a symbol of Germany's division and the cold war, was opened up, reuniting East and West.

East Germany. The farms, factories and businesses there, which were adapted to state control and supported by large subsidies, could not compete with those of the West. Unemployment soared as outmoded, overstaffed East German companies closed.

Other problems soon followed reunification. People in the former East Germany faced a steep rise in their cost of living because prices were no longer kept low through government controls. In the former West Germany, people suffered a decline in their standard of living as the government extended its expensive programmes of social support to millions more people and poured billions of pounds into updating industries in the East. The cost of investment in the former East Germany continues to be a challenge for the economy of Germany as a whole.

These economic troubles were deepened by the world-wide recession of the early 1990s. Germany also received millions of refugees from parts of south-east Europe, where the fall of communist governments had sparked violence. Despite these challenges, the country made steady progress in the task of unifying the economies and bringing together the citizens of East and West.

THE ADMINISTRATION

Germany is a federal republic, meaning that power is shared between a central elected authority and partly independent regional authorities. The republic is founded on a written **constitution** – called the **Basic Law** – that guarantees human rights and democratic government for its citizens. There are three levels of government: national, state and municipal. Principal political responsibilities are divided between federal and state governments.

The president

The president is the head of state and performs many ceremonial duties, representing Germany at important national and international events. He or she is elected every five years by a special assembly drawn from the German states and parliament's lower house. Although the president has little political power, the duties he or she performs, such as signing treaties and federal legislation, are vital to the daily affairs of the government.

Parliament and the chancellor

The parliament is where politicians meet to discuss events and issues, debate bills and pass new laws. The federal parliament has two houses: the **Bundestag** (lower house) and the **Bundesrat** (upper house). Of the

The Bundestag is elected every four years by German citizens aged eighteen years and over. During an election, citizens have two votes – one for their state parliament and another for the federal parliament.

The chart shows how Germany is governed. The president has little political power, which is in the hands of the chancellor and the federal and state governments.

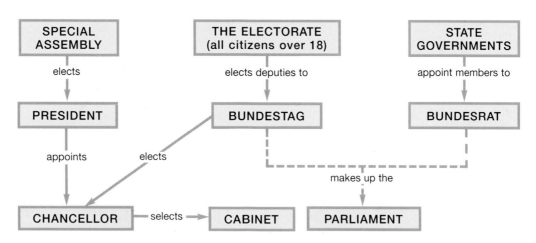

79

This glass dome, designed by British architect Sir Norman Foster (born 1935), tops the revamped Reichstag in Berlin. The building has been the home of the Bundestag since 1999.

The Bundesrat has 69 members, with each state sending from three to six representatives. More populous states send more members than those with smaller populations. The Bundestag has 603 seats, held by politicians from all regions of the country.

two houses, the Bundestag is the larger and more powerful. Its members create, debate and pass laws that affect all of Germany. They also decide on such important matters as defence, the budget and foreign affairs.

After an election, the members of the Bundestag elect the head of the government (chancellor). The candidate is first formally nominated by the president, but he or she is usually the leader of the party that has won the largest number of seats in the Bundestag. Once elected, the chancellor selects the ministers who will make up the government, and they are formally appointed by the president. Ministers are usually Bundestag members and come from the party or coalition of parties forming the largest voting bloc in the Bundestag.

The Bundesrat

The upper house of Germany's parliament is smaller and less powerful than the Bundestag, and members are selected from the governments of Germany's states. Each year, leadership of the Bundesrat alternates between the heads of the state governments. The Bundesrat helps Germany's states balance the national powers of the Bundestag. It reviews and votes on federal laws passed by the Bundestag, either approving them or raising objections and returning them to the lower house for debate.

The state governments

Each of Germany's sixteen states (*Länder*) has its own parliament, government and equivalent of the chancellor. The three city-states – Berlin, Hamburg and Bremen – have a mayor who also acts as state 'chancellor' and a municipal senate that serves as the state parliament. Each state creates regional laws concerning education, the environment, roads and health care, and commands a local police force.

Political parties

Germans vote for political parties that hold different opinions on how the country should be run. Similar parties exist at both national and state levels. The parties win seats in parliament according to the percentage of votes they get. The party that wins the most seats forms the government. A party must gain 5 per cent of the total votes in an election in order to hold seats. This system was set up to discourage small extremist parties from gaining control in parliament.

The major parties

Two parties dominate German politics: the Social Democratic Party (SPD) and the Christian Democratic Union (CDU). While the SPD favours more government controls on the economy and promotes social programmes, the CDU prefers less government involvement and minimal controls on private enterprise. Both parties, however, support close ties with the West and with NATO.

Other parties include the liberal Free Democratic Party (FDP); the Christian Social Union (CSU) – the CDU's sister party in Bavaria; Alliance 90/Greens – a union of former East German citizens' groups and the Greens, whose platform is dominated by environmental issues; the Party of Democratic Socialism, which formerly governed communist East Germany; and the right-wing Republican Party.

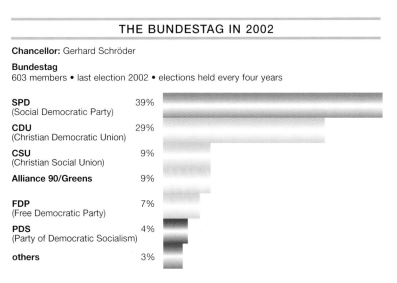

THE BUNDESTAG IN 2002

Chancellor: Gerhard Schröder

Bundestag
603 members • last election 2002 • elections held every four years

SPD (Social Democratic Party)	39%	
CDU (Christian Democratic Union)	29%	
CSU (Christian Social Union)	9%	
Alliance 90/Greens	9%	
FDP (Free Democratic Party)	7%	
PDS (Party of Democratic Socialism)	4%	
others	3%	

Elections to the Bundestag were held in 2002. The vote gave the SPD and Alliance 90/Greens coalition government a majority of just nine seats – the slimmest majority in postwar Germany. Gerhard Schröder of the SPD was re-elected as chancellor.

The economy

'… merely the result of honest endeavour on the part of a whole nation …'

20th-century politician Ludwig Erhard, on the German economic recovery

Despite its devastated condition at the end of World War Two (1939–45), the German economy has grown in leaps and bounds in the decades since to become one of the strongest in the world. Today, it ranks third after those of the USA and Japan. Along with the USA, Japan, France, Canada, the UK, Italy and Russia, Germany is a member of the Group of Eight. Known as G8 for short, these are the world's seven leading **industrial** countries plus Russia.

Germany's economic success rests not so much on natural resources or raw materials but on the country's location, skilled and motivated workforce, brilliant engineering and superb products. Germany is conveniently situated in the centre of the largest **open market** in the world – the **European Union** (EU). The country also borders the emerging (developing) markets of eastern Europe. German workers design and manufacture products with close attention to detail, and their goods have earned a reputation for high quality and reliable delivery. As a result, German products are in demand in many other countries, which leads to Germany's ranking as a leader in **exports** and makes foreign trade a major part of the country's economy. A number of German businesses rank in the global top ten of firms in their field. Among Germany's most important exports are motor vehicles and iron and steel products.

The power stations of the Ruhr Valley in western Germany fuel a huge industrial area that traditionally produces coal and steel.

FACT FILE

● Germany has a large immigrant population of more than 7 million. Of those, more than 2 million are Turkish citizens.

● In 2000, Germany ranked third in the world in each of industrial, manufacturing and services output.

● In 1999, the average annual earnings, before tax, of German workers were the equivalent of £30,413.

● In 2001, 96% of German households had a television set and 66% had a mobile phone.

● In 2001, 9.4% of the German working-age population were unemployed.

THE ECONOMY SINCE WORLD WAR TWO

When World War Two ended, German cities and towns lay buried under rubble. The country's roads, railways, bridges, power stations and communication lines were in ruins. Less than half of its factories were destroyed, but the prospects for German industry remained grim – there were no materials to work with and nothing with which to pay the workers.

While heavy industry plays an important part in Germany's export economy, services, such as banking, employ nearly two-thirds of the workforce. Very few Germans now work in agriculture.

The economic miracle

Within twenty years, **West Germany** had built the third-largest economy in the world. The recovery was labelled the *Wirtschaftswunder* (economic miracle). The economy's rapid growth can be attributed in large part to the hard labour of German workers. However, other factors played a part. The introduction of a new currency, the Deutsche Mark (German mark), in 1949 wiped out the country's debt and encouraged spending. In addition, as part of the **Marshall Plan** (see page 74), West Germany also began to receive millions of dollars in US aid. The West German government directed most of this aid into modernizing industries that promised long-term growth, such as mining, steel and transportation. As German goods quickly gained a reputation for high quality, demand for them increased, industry grew and West Germany's economy boomed.

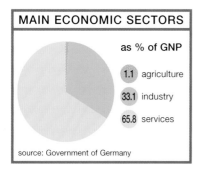

MAIN ECONOMIC SECTORS

as % of GNP

1.1	agriculture
33.1	industry
65.8	services

source: Government of Germany

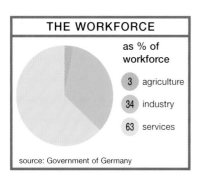

THE WORKFORCE

as % of workforce

3	agriculture
34	industry
63	services

source: Government of Germany

The East German economy

East Germany made a slower postwar economic recovery than the West did. Like other Soviet-bloc countries, East Germany had a planned **communist** economy. The government owned all the businesses and farms and decided what goods to produce, how many and how much they would cost. Everyone was guaranteed a job, and prices remained low because they were controlled by the government, which also set employees' wages.

Despite its benefits, the communist system had severe shortcomings. Companies did not compete to produce the best goods at the lowest prices, so many were inefficient and overstaffed. Product variety was limited, too, and government miscalculations sometimes led to shortages of goods.

> **In East Germany, a person could wait more than ten years for a new car, and twelve years or more for a telephone line.**

After reunification

Economic reunification was one of the first steps towards full reunification. On 1 July 1990, West Germany's Deutsche Mark replaced the East German currency. Shortly after, trade barriers between the East and West were lifted, and East Germany's price controls were removed. East Germans were shocked by the high prices they now had to pay for goods. To make matters worse, many East Germans were soon out of work. Their companies could not compete in the **capitalist** market against the more efficient West German firms.

Frankfurt is the financial heart of postwar Germany. Hundreds of banks have offices in the city.

To aid the process of reunification, the government set up an agency called the *Treuhandanstalt* (THA, or Trust Institution). Western firms were reluctant to invest in the East and privatize companies there because of the cost of upgrading plants, paying unemployment compensation and cleaning up pollution created by the old operations. After closing almost 2000 businesses, the THA tried to make investing in the East more attractive by offering incentives to buyers, including loans with little or no interest. Some major corporations began investing in industry in the East.

THE WORKFORCE

German workers have earned a global reputation for hard work, efficiency and skill. However, they are also expensive. German workers earn higher salaries than do their European and North American counterparts and also enjoy some of the most generous benefits in the world. For example, they can take as much as six weeks of paid holiday each year. Added to that, the German working week averages about 37 hours – the shortest among the industrialized nations. Generally, though, German workers accomplish the same amount of work in a shorter time than workers in other countries.

Works councils

German workers can comment on the running of the businesses where they work. Any company that employs more than five workers must establish a *Betriebsrat*, a council that represents employee interests in matters such as working hours, job training and company rules. The *Betriebsrat* must also be informed about hiring and firing, although it may lack the power to influence those decisions.

Women at work

The **Basic Law** (the German **constitution**) states that men and women should receive equal treatment, but equality remains rare in the workplace. Unlike almost all other Western nations, Germany lacks laws preventing discrimination against women. Although German women make up about 40 per cent of the workforce, they hold only 2 per cent of the top-level positions in business, banking and industry. Average salaries for men are generally 50 per cent higher than those for women.

Workers' unions

Unions have the important responsibility of negotiating rights and wages for the employees they represent. Each year, union officials meet with management to reach a wage agreement and renew the workers' contracts. In the event that an agreement cannot be reached, unions are far more likely to call for a work stoppage than a strike. During a work stoppage, which can last for minutes,

hours or days, the employees simply refuse to perform their jobs, but the employers must continue to pay them. However, during a strike, which is a formal, organized version of a work stoppage, the union must pay the workers.

Car workers strike for more pay at the Opel car factory at Rüsselsheim, south- west of Frankfurt.

In Germany, a strike takes place only if the employees' union and the employers' association are unable to reach an agreement and 75 per cent of the union members vote to strike. German unions maintain a relationship based on co-operation with employers rather than confrontation, and use strikes only as a last resort. German unions represent all workers within a particular industry rather than a single profession or trade. For example, all workers in mining companies belong to the miners' union, regardless of their job. This system eliminates squabbles over which union's members do which jobs in the workplace.

The government's role

Germany has a social market economy, which means businesses operate in a free market but not at the expense of citizens' well-being. Operating according to its motto – 'As little government as possible, as much government as necessary' – the government regulates business. It oversees the relationship between workers and business owners and tries to ensure a competitive, fair market by limiting monopolies, but it avoids direct involvement in fixing prices or wages.

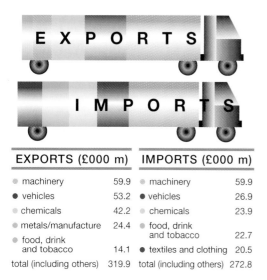

EXPORTS (£000 m)		IMPORTS (£000 m)	
machinery	59.9	machinery	59.9
vehicles	53.2	vehicles	26.9
chemicals	42.2	chemicals	23.9
metals/manufacture	24.4	food, drink and tobacco	22.7
food, drink and tobacco	14.1	textiles and clothing	20.5
total (including others)	319.9	total (including others)	272.8

source: Government of Germany

The diagram above shows Germany's imports and exports. The one below shows the country's main trading partners.

MAIN TRADING PARTNERS

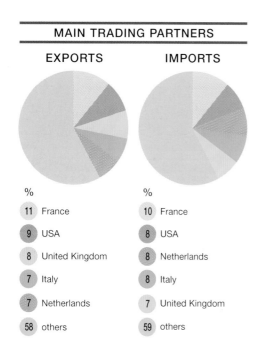

EXPORTS		IMPORTS	
%		%	
11	France	10	France
9	USA	8	USA
8	United Kingdom	8	Netherlands
7	Italy	8	Italy
7	Netherlands	7	United Kingdom
58	others	59	others

source: Government of Germany

FOREIGN TRADE

Foreign trade is the foundation on which much of Germany's economy is built. More than one-third of all goods and services produced by Germans are exported. Trade barriers, such as **tariffs**, make exporting difficult, and West Germany was a leader in the move towards an open European market. In 1957, with Belgium, France, Italy, Luxembourg and the Netherlands, West Germany founded the European Economic Community (EEC), or Common Market. Countries in the EEC eventually eliminated trade barriers among themselves, set pricing and aid limits for some industries and set tariffs for goods imported from non-member countries. Over time, the number of EEC members grew.

The EEC was part of an overall institution called simply the European Community (EC). In November 1993, the EC became the European Union (EU). Among the aims of the EU was the establishment of a single European currency, which would enable the EU countries to trade as a single bloc. Supporters of the single currency believed this capability would help the EU to compete more successfully in the world market. In 1999, twelve EU members, including Germany, adopted the single currency, called the euro. At first, however, the euro was used only for international trading. In January 2002, the euro replaced the national currencies of the EU countries that had adopted it.

MAJOR SECTORS

Economists divide a country's economy into sectors. Each sector covers a type of economic activity, such as agriculture and industry. Different countries are stronger in some sectors than they are in others.

Agriculture

Agriculture underwent enormous changes in western Germany during the 20th century, mainly because of the decreasing profitability of smaller farms and the increasing use of farm machinery. Until mid-century, most farms were small, family-run businesses. As government aid decreased, though, many farmers began to doubt that their farms could survive. Many still work their land but do so only part-time, relying instead on other jobs as their main source of income. Some have sold their property to operators of larger farms.

Since 1950, about three-quarters of farm-workers in western Germany have left the fields to pursue work in other industries. The shrinking number of farms and farmworkers has not created a shortage of produce or live-stock, however. In 1950, most farms produced enough food for just ten people. Today, farms of the same size can feed about 70 people, mainly as a result of improvements in seeds, fertilizers and machinery.

In the former East Germany, farming was very different from in the West. Whereas most West German farms were small, family-owned businesses, farms in East Germany were vast enterprises. There were two main types of East German farms: people's farms, called *Volkseigenen Gutern* (VEG), which were owned entirely by the government and worked by government employ-ees, and co-operative farms, called *Landwirtschaftliche Produktionsgenossenschäfte* (LPGs), which were owned

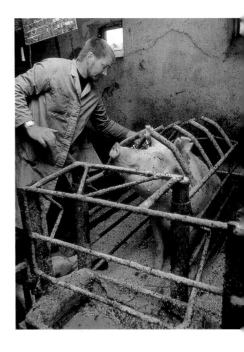

A farmer tends his pigs in Zwickau in the former East Germany. German farmers raise more pigs than any other type of livestock.

In the 1980s, just 5 per cent of West German farms were larger than 50 hectares (124 acres). East German arable farms averaged 4570 hectares (11,292 acres).

HOW GERMANY
USES ITS LAND

*German crop land is
concentrated in the
centre of the country,
while pasture land
lies mostly near
the northern coasts.*

crop land

forest

pasture

*This diagram shows
how German land
is divided among
various uses.*

jointly by the government and the people who worked them. Their crops were purchased by the government at rates much higher than – sometimes more than double – those in the West. After reunification, the modernization of farming in the East began. This included a good deal of streamlining and a sharp fall in the numbers of former East Germans who were working in farming.

Forestry

Although forests cover more than one-third of Germany, the forestry industry contributes a very small amount to the country's economy. More than a million trees are cut down each year, supplying roughly half of Germany's requirements. The balance of timber needs is met by **imports** from Austria and Scandinavia.

While the government encourages logging companies to replant more trees than they cut, Germany's forests are still endangered. More than half of all Germany's trees are suffering from *Waldsterben* (wood death) as a result of air pollution and **acid rain** (see box page 31).

Fishing

Fishing was once an important source of income for the people of northern Germany. The industry was focused mainly in the North and Baltic seas, and had fleets in the Atlantic Ocean off the coasts of Ireland, Great Britain and Greenland. Since 1970, however, it has been in

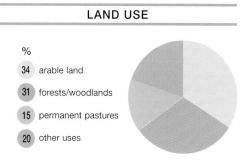

LAND USE

%

34 arable land

31 forests/woodlands

15 permanent pastures

20 other uses

source: Government of Germany

decline. Catches have decreased in size because of reduced fish stocks and competition with fleets from other countries. Although the North Sea herring fishery has diminished, herring remains an important part of the German diet. Shrimp and mussels are still a source of income on the mudflats of the North Sea coast.

Manufacturing

Manufacturing is German industry's largest and strongest sector. Vehicles, chemicals, pharmaceuticals, machinery, precision tools and instruments and electrical equipment are the most important products. The country's largest corporations produce these high-quality, labour-intensive goods and include Daimler-Benz, Volkswagen, BMW, BASF, Bayer, Hoechst, Siemens and SAP.

A fisherman sorts his herring catch on the island of Usedom, just off the Baltic coast of Mecklenburg-West Pomerania.

  German industry realized some time ago that, with its highly skilled but expensive labour force, it could not successfully compete with Asian manufacturers, whose

Beer and wine

Germany produces many world-famous beers. It sells more beer within Europe than any other country and holds more than 10% of the world market for beer – a share second only to that of the USA. German brewers produce more than 11,500 million litres (2530 million gallons) of beer each year, employing 65,000 people and exporting to more than 150 countries. Brewing is the second-largest sector of the agricultural industry after dairy products.

Germany also produces wine. Historians believe German wine-making goes back to 100 BC, when Romans first brought vines to the area. Today, there are about 100,000 hectares (247,100 acres) of vineyards, located mainly along the valleys of the Rhine, Neckar and Mosel rivers. Germany is one of the most northerly wine-making countries. White wine forms the bulk of production, many of the best German wines being produced from the Riesling grape.

lower costs enable them to mass-produce goods cheaply. To survive, many German manufacturers shifted their focus to specialized or sophisticated items produced to the highest possible quality. Some manufacturers have found success by identifying a specific type of product for which there is a demand and then tailoring their business to supply it.

Volkswagen – the people's car

Volkswagen was founded in 1938 by Adolf Hitler to produce a cheap *Volkswagen* (people's car). The company established its first plant in Wolfsburg, and the original model, eventually known as the Beetle, was designed by Ferdinand Porsche. Millions of Germans invested in special savings stamps that were to earn them a car once the factory began manufacturing them. When World War Two broke out, however, the company built vehicles for the military instead.

When the **Allies** occupied Germany at the end of the war, British forces took over the company, employing its former workers and engineers to service their vehicles and to build Volkswagens from remaining parts. In 1949, the British handed over control of the factory to the newly formed

government of West Germany. The factory employed over 10,000 people and produced more than 46,000 cars in 1949. The government soon brought a new manager, Heinz Nordoff, to the factory, and he revolutionized the company.

At first, people in other countries had reservations about the Beetle – they thought it ugly and disliked buying a product built by a former enemy. In the end, however, they were swayed by the car's affordability and complete service package. For decades, the Beetle was the world's best-loved car, shattering the Ford Model T's record as the best-selling car of all time. Today, Volkswagen makes a variety of models, including the new model Beetle (pictured below) and the Golf, Europe's most popular small car. Volkswagen also owns the Audi car company.

MAJOR INDUSTRIES

The map shows the most important industries found in Germany's major cities and the Ruhr Valley industrial area.

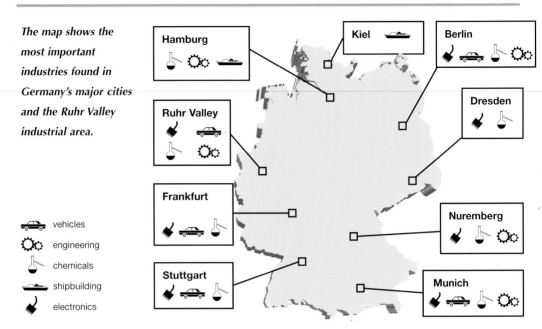

vehicles
engineering
chemicals
shipbuilding
electronics

Finance and banking

Germany's central bank is the Bundesbank, based in Frankfurt. It is not open to the public but is similar to the Bank of England. Among the Bundesbank's tasks is the regulation of the amount of money in circulation in Germany. Each state has a branch of the central bank. Before reunification, East Germany also had a central bank. When East and West were reunified economically on 1 July 1990, the East German banking system was taken over by the Bundesbank.

Raw materials

Although raw materials account for little of its economy in overall terms, Germany is the largest European producer of potash, which is used to make fertilizer, chemicals, soap and glass. Huge deposits are mined in the North German Plain and in the upper Rhine and Fulda valleys. Besides potash, Germany's natural wealth includes coal, lignite (brown coal) and salt, as well as some oil and natural gas. There are also iron-ore

Germans can choose from hundreds of banks, depending on the services required. According to 1999 figures, the largest German banks were Deutsche Bank, HypoVereinsbank and Dresdner Bank.

deposits, although iron-ore mining has declined since the 1970s. Today, Germany relies on imports to supply most of its iron ore, as well as other materials needed for manufacturing, such as bauxite, manganese, phosphate and tin.

Most of the former East Germany's energy came from lignite (brown coal) dug from open-cast mines such as this one near Leipzig.

Energy sources

Although Germany has few energy sources of its own, the country is the world's fifth-largest energy consumer. It relies heavily on imports of crude oil and natural gas, the bulk of which comes from the Middle East, the North Sea and from Russia and other former Soviet countries. Germany's reliance on natural gas is likely to increase in the future as the country tries to reduce its dependence on lignite (brown coal). Although Germany has huge deposits of lignite, burning it causes environmental damage. Germany is also exploring the use of wind and solar power as a means of reducing its consumption of polluting energy sources.

ENERGY SOURCES

%

67 oil, gas, coal and diesel

30 nuclear power

3 hydroelectric power and others

source: Government of Germany

The diagram shows Germany's major fuels and the proportion of the country's energy each type generates.

A nuclear power

In the late 1960s, West Germany developed a nuclear energy programme. The intentions were to reduce the country's reliance on imports, its use of polluting energy sources and the cost of electricity. Today, nuclear power is produced in 27 power stations and accounts for more than one-third of Germany's energy production. The energy source has long been controversial because of environmental and safety concerns, however, and many protests have occurred. Five Soviet-produced reactors in the former East Germany have been closed down because of design flaws, poor materials and inadequate maintenance.

Communications

Germany has an advanced communications system. A government agency, the Bundespost, runs the country's network of postal, telephone and telegraph services. The Bundespost is the largest service firm in Europe and is expensive to use. Critics complain that the agency is too slow and old-fashioned because of its huge size and monopoly. They suggest that competition would increase innovation in communications technology while reducing prices.

Transportation

Germany's transportation system comprises air, water, rail and road networks. When Germany was reunified, the West had a more up-to-date system than the East. Modernization pro-grammes were begun to equalize the situation and to reopen and improve east–west routes.

TRANSPORTATION

In general, Germany has a sophisticated transportation system based on networks of waterways, roads, railways and air routes. However, east–west links between the former West and East Germany were not developed during the years of division. Also, much of the transportation infrastructure in the former East Germany required enormous investment to bring it to a level equal to that of the West. After reunification, programmes were introduced to address both of these problems.

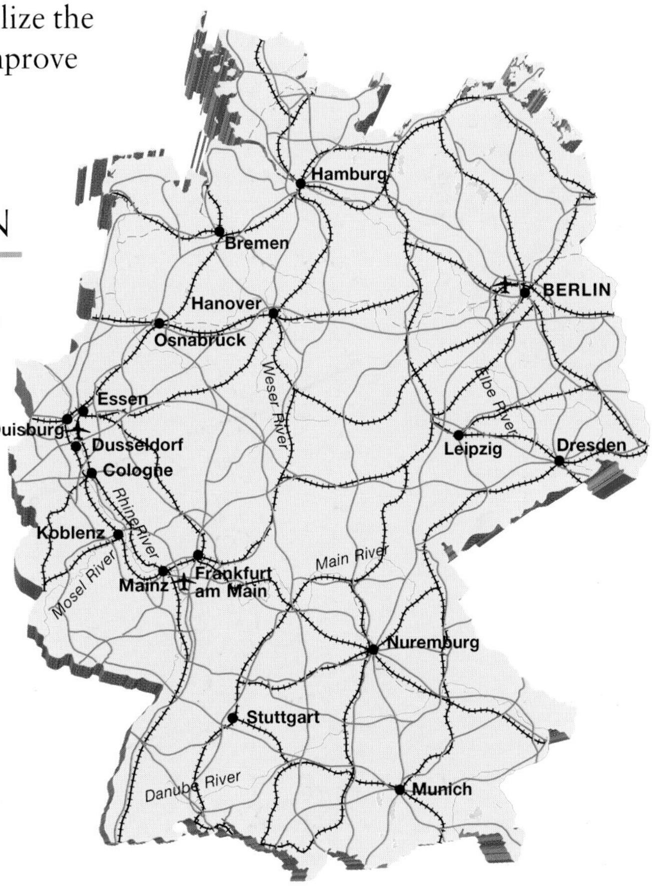

——— major roads

+++++ railways

——— major waterways

✈ major airports

Germany has 7467 km (4640 miles) of waterways, 239,741 km (148,972 miles) of major roads, including autobahns (motorways), and 45,942 km (28,547 miles) of railways.

To encourage commuters to leave their cars at home, the German government has modernized its city rail systems. In addition, in many large cities, a single ticket allows passengers to switch among the underground, tram and bus networks.

Waterways

Since earliest times, Germany's many rivers have acted as water highways, linking communities otherwise separated by difficult terrain. Settlements along rivers were connected to one another as well as to ports along the North and Baltic seas. The rivers helped to make Germany into a key centre for trade between Europe, Asia and the Middle East.

Today, several networks of modern canals enable barges, boats and ships to pass easily between different rivers to reach the country's industrial centres, many of which were built alongside rivers. Together, Germany's rivers and canals carry more than 25 per cent of all the country's freight.

Railways

Germany's first railway, a 5-kilometre (3-mile) stretch in Bavaria that linked Nuremberg and Furth, opened for service in 1835. Since then, the country has added more than 46,000 kilometres (28,500 miles) of tracks and now boasts one of the world's most advanced rail systems.

The German national railway is Deutsche Bahn, which has been modernized in recent years, switching many of its lines from coal and diesel to cleaner electric power. Besides standard passenger trains, it also offers special services. One such service, the InterCityExpress (ICE), makes hourly trips between major cities at speeds of up to 280 kilometres (174 miles) per hour, while the EuroCity (EC) express trains provide high-speed links between Germany and the rest of Europe. Despite its modern system, Deutsche Bahn has faced increased competition from road transportation for both freight and passengers.

Roads

Germans developed the earliest practical car engines and cars, and today make some of the most respected vehicles in the world. At 516 cars for every 1000 people,

Germany has the sixth-highest car ownership in the world. A remarkable 45 million vehicles, or 66 cars per kilometre, travel German roadways – more per kilometre than anywhere else in Europe. Lorries, more than any other means of transportation, move the most freight.

Many sections of autobahns have no posted speed limit, and drivers may reach speeds of 200 km/h (125 mph).

Air transit

Germany's national airline, Lufthansa, was formed in 1926 to provide passengers with regular flights to the rest of Europe. Dissolved at the end of World War Two, it was re-established in the mid-1950s and today is one of the most important airlines in the world, offering flights to more than 85 countries.

It has only been possible to fly between eastern and western Germany since 1989.

More than 800 million travellers use Germany's airports each year. Western Germany has a number of international airports, the largest and most important of which is in Frankfurt. Schöneberg in the east of Berlin is the only eastern airport with connections to the West.

The autobahns

Germany's famous motorways, such as the example pictured here, are called autobahns (*Autobahne* in German). They are some of the fastest, longest and busiest roads in the world. Connecting northern and southern Europe, they provide crucial links between industrial centres inside and outside Germany.

The autobahns – the first major paved roads in the world – were constructed during the **Nazi** regime in the 1930s to create work for some of Germany's unemployed labourers. By 1945, there were about 1400 km (870 miles) of autobahns; today, there are more than 11,000 km (6835 miles). The German government has expanded the autobahn network to accommodate the increasing number of vehicles on the roads, but massive traffic jams are still common because of construction, roadworks, bad weather, rush hours and accidents.

Arts and living

'Even bad books are books, and therefore sacred.'

20th-century writer Günter Grass

Most Germans underwent tremendous changes in their lifestyles, values and beliefs in the 20th century. Many of these changes were brought on by the two world wars. Survivors were left to rebuild their towns, cities and country. They also had to come to terms first with the Treaty of Versailles at the end of World War One, and later with the atrocities committed during the **Nazi** era of the 1930s and 1940s.

Under their regime, the Nazis promoted traditional German lifestyles and customs in their propaganda. As a result, these values became tainted in the eyes of most Germans when the Nazis were expelled from power. In an attempt to put the past behind them, many Germans embraced modern tastes, values and lifestyles that were free of disagreeable associations, and worked almost single-mindedly to revitalize their country's economy.

At the beginning of the 21st century, after decades of hard work, Germans' values and daily lives are once again undergoing a transformation. Lifestyles in all parts of Germany have changed since the mid-1980s, reflecting a shift in priorities from a work-oriented society to one where leisure has increased in importance. Because Germans enjoy one of the highest standards of living in the world, they are able to explore a variety of pursuits, expanding their tastes in fashion, food, music and other areas.

The interior of the Wallfahrtskirche, at Birnau on the Bodensee, is an example of the ornate rococo style that emerged in Germany in the 18th century.

FACT FILE

- Germany's history as a patchwork of loosely bound political units gave rise to a rich and varied cultural tradition. The country's regions are home to varying dialects, foods and folk celebrations.

- Germany has one of the lowest birth rates in the world – 1.4 children per woman.

- Germans spend an average of 20% of their income on leisure activities.

- The average age for German men marrying for the first time is 30 years and 4 months; for German women, it is 27 years and 10 months.

THE ARTS

The Germans have a rich cultural and artistic heritage, which includes some of the world's most brilliant musicians, writers, architects and thinkers. German heritage encompasses an area greater than the borders of present-day Germany and includes German-speaking artists in Austria, the Czech **Republic** and other central European countries. This cultural tradition spans centuries of major European artistic movements, including the Gothic, Renaissance and Baroque periods, as well as romanticism and modernism. It reflects shifts in values and ideas that have taken place during this time.

The arts are an important part of life in Germany. This fact is demonstrated both by the generous financial support provided by governments and by the sheer number of cultural venues in the country. Every city and most towns have an opera company, orchestra and sometimes even a ballet company. Most Germans regard the arts and other cultural activities not only as entertainment but also as a means of self-improvement.

Home of musical genius

For centuries, music has been Germany's first love. Germany and the German-speaking country of Austria have produced many classical Western composers. The impressive list spans ten centuries, stretching all the way back to St Hildegard (1098–1179). A Benedictine nun from Bingen, a town on the Rhine River, St Hildegard wrote early religious music.

The great years of German music began in the Baroque period, with the emergence of composers such as Johann Sebastian Bach (1685–1750) and George Frideric Handel (1685–1759), although the latter lived in England from 1712. Both wrote huge quantities of music, instrumental and vocal, religious and otherwise.

During music's classical period, from about 1750 to about 1825, types of work such as the concerto, sonata and symphony took form. The German world produced

The Gothic period extended from the 12th to the 16th centuries; the Renaissance, from the 14th to the 16th; the Baroque, from the 17th to the 18th; romanticism, from the late 18th to the end of the 19th; and modernism began in the 20th century.

More than 100 local and regional music festivals take place in Germany, featuring all kinds of music from opera to jazz and folk.

Beethoven

Ludwig van Beethoven (1770–1827) is universally regarded as a genius and possibly the greatest composer in history. His works did much to increase the status of music, previously regarded as inferior to literature and painting. His compositions challenged the commonly held view of music as nothing more than 'the art of pleasing sounds' by demonstrating the emotional power of the medium.

Beethoven is almost as remarkable for certain details of his personal life as for his musical accomplishment. Born in Bonn, Beethoven moved to Vienna in the 1790s to be taught by the great Austrian composer Franz Joseph Haydn (1732–1809). Beethoven became a virtuoso pianist, only to be faced, in about 1800, with the harsh fact that he was becoming deaf. He continued to perform until the condition forced him to stop in 1814.

As he played fewer public performances, Beethoven devoted more of his energy to composing. Many of his masterpieces were created in this later period of his life. These works included the Ninth Symphony, which contains a setting to music of the 'Ode to Joy', a poem by the German writer Friedrich von Schiller (1759–1805).

Beethoven died on 26 March 1827 after a long illness. Many thousands attended his funeral. His legacy of nine symphonies, numerous concertos, sonatas, one opera – *Fidelio* – and other musical works have enriched the world. Their intense emotion, attention to design and powerful beauty inspired subsequent generations of artists in various media.

As many as 146 professional orchestras enrich the cultural life of towns and cities in Germany. Many of these orchestras perform several concerts each week. The Berlin Philharmonic Orchestra is the most famous.

three geniuses in this time – Franz Joseph Haydn (1732–1809), Wolfgang Amadeus Mozart (1756–91), both of whom were Austrian, and Ludwig van Beethoven (1770–1827). Their vast output of music includes Mozart's comic opera masterpiece *The Marriage of Figaro*, Haydn's massive religious work *The Creation* and Beethoven's mighty Ninth Symphony.

Many historians see Beethoven as a link between the classical period and romanticism, a movement that lasted until the end of the 19th century and was influenced by emotion instead of order. Among the greats of the romantic period was Richard Wagner (1813–83), who wrote numerous operas based on German myths and legends. Franz Schubert (1797–1828), Felix Mendelssohn (1809–47), Robert Schumann (1810–56) and Johannes Brahms (1833–97) were other highly gifted German romantic composers.

Literature

Germany's literature first blossomed in the Middle Ages. Roving poets called *Minnesänger* (love singers) sang love poems at the courts of German nobles. Two of Germany's greatest medieval poets were Wolfram von Eschenbach and Gottfried von Strassburg. Both wrote long epic poems in the 13th century about knights and ladies. These poems are full of magic and pageantry.

This illustration of the Nibelungenlied shows Queen Kriemhild being taken to King Etzel (Attila) of the Huns, whom she is to marry.

No one knows who wrote the most famous epic of all – the *Nibelungenlied* (*Song of the Nibelungs*). This epic combines pagan legends, myths and songs with a historical event of the 5th century – the destruction of the Burgundians (a Germanic tribe) in the

The brothers Grimm

The two Grimm brothers, Jakob Ludwig Karl (1785–1863) and Wilhelm Karl (1786–1859) are famous for their collections of folktales. Almost 200 years after it was published, their first collection, *Kinder und Hausmärchen*, known as *Grimms' Fairy Tales*, is still read and enjoyed by families around the world. It is one of the world's most frequently translated books. The brothers travelled the country, asking people to recount stories and songs that had been passed down through the generations in their families. In total, they gathered about 200 tales, of which the most famous are 'Rumpelstiltskin', 'Snow Drop' (or 'Snow White') and 'Hansel and Gretel'.

Rhineland region by Attila and his Huns. It tells the story of the hero, Siegfried, his wife, Queen Kriemhild, her brother, King Gunther, and his wife, Queen Brunhild. Greed, pride, treachery and revenge intermingle as these characters come to a violent end. The tale was the basis of Wagner's series of operas known as the Ring Cycle, and was drawn upon by J. R. R. Tolkien in his saga *The Lord of the Rings*.

The next glorious period of German literature occurred in the late 18th and early 19th centuries. It is often called the *Goethezeit* (Goethe time) because Johann Wolfgang von Goethe (1749–1832) was its towering figure. It was also the time, however, of the playwright and poet Friedrich von Schiller (1759–1805), one of Goethe's friends in the great literary city of Weimar. Schiller's plays inspired romantic artists across Europe. His works, such as *William Tell*, *Mary Stuart* and *Don Carlos*, are exciting dramas about illustrious heroes of history and are particularly concerned with the question 'What is freedom?'

Other German writers of this period include the playwright Gotthold Ephraim Lessing (1729–81), the poet Friedrich Hölderlin (1770–1843) and the short-story writer and dramatist Heinrich von Kleist (1777–1811). Their works are among Germany's *Klassiker* (classics) – the accepted masterpieces of literature.

Besides basing his Ring Cycle on the *Nibelungenlied*, the composer Richard Wagner drew on several other German epic poems for his operas, among them *Parsifal* and *Tristan and Isolde*.

103

Johann Wolfgang von Goethe

Johann Wolfgang von Goethe (1749–1832) is widely acclaimed as Germany's greatest writer and one of the giants of world literature. Goethe not only wrote plays, poems, novels and short stories but worked as a statesman and scientist as well. He was a botanist, too, and also produced a treatise on colours and light.

Goethe's most famous work is *Faust*, on which he worked almost all his adult life. This two-part play tells the story of a scholar whose quest for knowledge tempts him into a pact with the devil. The play comprises poetry and songs as well as prose. Goethe is pictured below in a 1787 painting by Johann Tischbein (1751–1829), entitled *Goethe in the Campagna*.

At the turn of the 20th century, many writers shifted from large, philosophical themes to the politics and social conditions of Germany. Thomas Mann (1875–1955), for example, wrote long, thoughtful novels, such as *Buddenbrooks*, which charts the success and the downfall of a merchant family, and *The Magic Mountain*, about a mountain hospital for people suffering from tuberculosis.

During the 1930s, the Nazis imprisoned many writers or drove them into exile. The Nazis also ceremonially burnt books by writers they regarded as 'undesirable'. The German-born novelist and poet Hermann Hesse (1877–1962) wrote: 'He who burns books, will burn people.'

One German writer who went into exile after the rise of the Nazis was the play-wright Bertolt Brecht (1898–1956), whose works were inspired by his **communist** ideals. One of Brecht's most famous plays is *Mother Courage*, in which he showed the trials of a mother trying to keep herself and her chil-dren alive during the bloody Thirty Years' War (1618–48). Brecht also worked with the German-born composer Kurt Weill (1900–50), producing operettas such as *The Threepenny Opera*. Like Brecht, Weill fled Nazi Germany and settled in the USA.

The end of Nazi rule in 1945 marked a new begin-ning for German literature, as writers such as Günter Grass (born 1927) – winner of the Nobel Prize for Literature in 1999 – and Heinrich Böll (1917–85) – winner of the prize in 1972 – struggled to come to terms with the horrors of World War Two (1939–45), Nazi atrocities and the guilt carried by German citizens. These writers have since won a huge following outside Germany. Among the most prominent modern German writers are Siegfried Lenz (born 1926), Peter Weiss (1916–82) and Uwe Johnson (1934–84), all from the former **West Germany,** and Stefan Heym (born 1913), Anna Seghers (1900–83) and Christa Wolf (born 1929) from the former **East Germany.**

A poem by Hölderlin

Friedrich Hölderlin's poem 'Half of Life' describes a romantic scene in summer and winter.

With yellow pears
And full of wild roses,
The land into the lake hangs down.
You loving swans,
Drunk with kisses,
Drop your heads into the holy and
*   sober water.*
But oh, where shall I find
When winter comes, the flowers, and where
The sunshine,
And shade of the earth?
The walls loom
Speechless and cold, in the wind
Weathercocks clatter.

Hermann Hesse, Heinrich Böll, Thomas Mann and Günter Grass are among the German writers who have been honoured with the Nobel Prize for Literature.

German philosophers

Germany has produced some of the world's most famous and influential thinkers. Immanuel Kant (1724–1804) and Georg Wilhelm Friedrich Hegel (1770–1831) evolved a philosophy known as idealism. Idealism stressed the importance of the human mind in creating reality. In other words, people cannot know the world as it really is but only as their senses and minds allow them to perceive it. Some idealists even believed that reality did not exist at all but was all a creation of the mind.

Arthur Schopenhauer (1788–1860) had different views. He believed that people were driven by a mysterious, unconscious and aimless force he called 'will'. Friedrich Nietzsche (1844–1900) developed this idea. However, for him the will was not aimless but was a creative 'will to power' that pushed people towards a higher, purer way of living.

For Karl Marx (1818–83), it was not the mind or the will that was important but economics. He argued that throughout history, insoluble problems had caused economic systems to break down and be replaced. In the case of **capitalism**, he predicted that technology would increase efficiency, which would create unemployment and poverty. Revolution would follow, and **socialism** would replace capitalism.

German art

Early German art can be seen in the illuminated (illustrated) manuscripts of the 9th century. Gothic panel painting emerged around 1300, and there were important centres in Saxony and Bavaria. At Augsburg the ruling Habsburg family employed Hans Holbein the Elder (*c*.1465–1524). His son, Holbein the Younger (1497/8–1543), was an important figure in the development of oil painting. One of the greatest German artists was Albrecht Dürer (1471–1528). Dürer brought the ideas of the Italian **Renaissance** to Germany. He was one of the first to sign his own paintings. Previously, painters were often thought of simply as craftsmen, working in guild systems where their work was unsigned and they were not given any special honour. Dürer, however, was very proud of his paintings and believed an artist's gifts were God-given.

In the early 19th century, the painter Caspar David Friedrich (1774–1840) tried to create works that were truly German. His paintings often depict vast, beautiful landscapes, such as rocky beaches, snowy mountains or thick, green forests (see above opposite). One of his best-known works is the altarpiece *The Cross in the Mountains*, now in Dresden.

Caspar David Friedrich's Mountain Landscape *shows his impressive command of perspective and the romantic view of Germany that he popularized.*

German artists were among the pioneers of modern art. At the beginning of the 20th century, artists such as Emil Nolde (1867–1956), Ernst Kirchner (1880–1938), Paula Modersohn-Becker (1876–1907) and Käthe Kollwitz (1867–1945) painted bold, colourful pictures and made black-and-white woodcuts of German cities, landscapes and people. Some, such as Kollwitz, were inspired by communist ideas; others, such as Nolde – who painted lonely seascapes around the Frisian Islands – were inspired by religious or mystical feelings. Emil Nolde's real name was Emil Hansen, and he took his pseudonym, Nolde, from his place of birth.

Architecture

The best examples from early German architecture are religious buildings. Aachen Cathedral's Palatine Chapel, begun in about 796, is a fine early medieval building (see page 53). The cathedral at Worms, begun in the 11th century, is in the Romanesque style, with characteristic rounded arches, while Cologne Cathedral, begun in 1248, has the pointed arches of the Gothic style. Later styles can be seen in palaces and monuments.

A highly elaborate style of non-religious Renaissance architecture developed around the valley of the Weser River in Hesse, Lower Saxony and Westphalia. This style was known as Weser Renaissance.

The Bauhaus

German design is renowned around the world for its clean lines, functionality and lack of decoration. Its style owes a lot to the famous school of art and design known as the Bauhaus ('building house'). The school was founded in Weimar in 1919 by the architect Walter Gropius (1883–1969). Its workshops produced revolutionary designs for ordinary household objects, such as chairs, tables and kettles. One of the Bauhaus' central principles was that an object's function should determine its form. Ornamentation of any kind was

considered distasteful because it served no practical function. The Bauhaus remained in Weimar from 1919 to 1925, when it moved to Dessau. In 1932, it moved to Berlin, before being closed by Hitler in 1933.

The mid-18th-century Sanssouci Palace at Potsdam is in the ornate rococo style, and Berlin's Brandenburg Gate, built towards the end of the 18th century, is neoclassical. The Bauhaus architects of the early 20th century created their own modern style, often using materials such as steel and glass. The Nazi period marked a return to monumental neoclassical architecture.

The New National Gallery in Berlin, built from 1962 to 1968, was designed by Ludwig Mies van der Rohe (1886–1969), formerly one of the leaders of the Bauhaus movement.

The media

Germany is home to more than 410 newspapers, ranging from local weeklies to big-city dailies, all of which are guaranteed freedom of expression under the **Basic Law.**

There are three public television channels that broadcast German documentaries, news, cultural programmes and political commentaries. Channels One and Two feature national programmes while Channel Three broadcasts local programming. Since the 1980s, when private corporations won the right to broadcast, other stations have become increasingly popular. Cable networks now offer more than seventeen channels.

DAILY LIFE

Most Germans live in cities and towns, mainly in rented apartments. Those who live in the countryside mostly have houses with small farms. They usually work these farms part-time to grow fresh foods for their family and supplement their income.

Recreation and sports

Most Germans take their recreation seriously – perhaps because leisure time is fairly new to them. Thirty years ago, German workers had the longest working week of any Western nation, regularly putting in 45 to 48 hours. In the 1970s, their working week decreased to 40 hours, and it has since shrunk to the shortest among the **industrialized** nations – about 37 hours.

One of the most popular leisure pursuits is watching and playing sports – one in three Germans belongs to a sports club. Football is by far the most popular sport. The German Football Federation (DFB) is the largest sports association in Germany, with more than 5 million members. A professional match can attract thousands of spectators. The second-favourite sport after football is gymnastics, while tennis, sailing, skiing, cycling, hiking, canoeing and rowing are all popular. Other pastimes include taking drives, visiting friends, reading and watching television.

Health and welfare

Germans value their health and welfare system, which is one of the most generous and comprehensive in the world. Even so, many are concerned over erosion of their social benefits. Since reunification, the system has been under enormous strain because the number of

In Boris Becker and Michael Stich, Germany produced two major tennis champions. In the women's game, Steffi Graf dominated women's tennis for much of the 1990s, with 22 Grand Slam singles titles.

Germany's football team has a world-class reputation in international competitions.

German social security provides accident insurance, unemployment benefits and pensions. The system is funded by contributions from employers, employees and the government.

EDUCATIONAL ATTENDANCE

further (university)	32%
secondary school	97%
primary school	100%

people drawing on it has increased dramatically. Job losses in the former East Germany have led to massive spending on unemployment benefits and retraining programmes. In response, the government has had to raise taxes and impose spending limits on drugs and other areas of medical care. Increasingly, Germans have purchased private health insurance.

Education

Because it relies on a highly skilled workforce, Germany places great emphasis on education and **vocational training**. Children attend school from Monday to Saturday. An average school day begins at 8 a.m. for pupils and finishes at about midday. Pupils then return home for lunch, and work on homework or play sports in the afternoon.

Most children begin attending their first school (*Grundschule*) at the age of six. Four years later, they switch to one of three types of secondary school. Teachers advise parents and pupils on which type of secondary schooling would best meet pupils' needs, abilities and future plans.

Students planning to enter the workforce with a specific skill attend a *Hauptschule*. There, they study general subjects such as maths, natural science, social science and a foreign language. Students attend until the age of fifteen or sixteen, when they go on to further vocational training, which includes skills training in the workplace. Young Germans who would like to work in commerce or administration attend a *Realschule* after leaving their first school. To improve their career prospects, these students then follow a further study programme at a technical school.

Students hoping to go to university must first spend nine years at a *Gymnasium*, which they start at the age of eleven. They study a wide range of subjects, including arts, literature, technology, sciences and maths. Students must pass an exam called the *Abitur* before gaining

How to say ...

German is the official language and is spoken by the vast majority of people in Germany. Different regions have different dialects, and Germans sometimes have trouble understanding one another's accents and slang. Standard, or high, German (*Hochdeutsch*) is used for writing, and when spoken does not have the regionalized accents of the dialects. The words and phrases below are translated in *Hochdeutsch*.

Please   *Bitte* (bitter)

Thank you   *Danke* (danker)

Hello   *Hallo* (hal-oh)

Goodbye   *Auf Wiedersehen* (owf vee-der-zay-en)

Yes   *Ja* (yah)   No   *Nein* (nighn)

How are you?   *Wie geht es Ihnen?* (vee geeht ess eenen?)

Sorry   *Verzeihung* (fehrtsighung)

Do you speak English?   *Sprechen Sie Englisch?* (sprekhen zee english?)

I don't understand   *Ich verstehe nicht* (ikh fehrshtayer nikht)

What is your name?   *Wie heissen Sie?* (vee highssen zee?)

My name is ...   *Ich heisse ...* (ikh highsser)

Mr   *Herr* (hair)

Mrs   *Frau* (frow)

Miss   *Fräulein* (froyline)

Numbers

One   *eins* (ighns)

Two   *zwei* (tsvigh)

Three   *drei* (drigh)

Four   *vier* (feer)

Five   *fünf* (fewnf)

Six   *sechs* (zeks)

Seven   *sieben* (zeeben)

Eight   *acht* (akht)

Nine   *neun* (noyn)

Ten   *zehn* (tsayn)

Days of the week

Sunday   *Sonntag* (zontahg)

Monday   *Montag* (montahg)

Tuesday   *Dienstag* (deenstahg)

Wednesday   *Mittwoch* (mitvokh)

Thursday   *Donnerstag* (donnerstahg)

Friday   *Freitag* (frightahg)

Saturday   *Samstag* (zamstahg)

entrance to one of the country's universities. A university degree is often the basis for a profession. In the late 1800s and early 1900s, Germany developed one of the world's most respected university systems. The system's reputation has come into question, however, as a result of the high numbers of students now attending university. Many people argue that overcrowding, underfunding and too few lecturers have lowered standards.

The idea of the kindergarten was first developed in Germany. The word literally means 'children-garden'.

Pork is Germany's favourite meat – Germans consume more of it per capita than any other nation.

Germans produce more than 200 varieties of bread and almost as many types of sausage.

Guten apetit!

Germans are renowned for their hearty appetites and for liking heavy, starchy foods. Their tastes have slowly shifted in the past 50 years, however, as they have become more conscious of the healthy benefits of fruits, vegetables and other light fare.

Most Germans eat four or five meals a day. Breakfast (*Frühstück*), eaten early in the morning, typically consists of bread with jam, cheese, meats and fruit. A second breakfast (*zweite Frühstück*), usually made up of a sandwich or two, may be eaten at about 9 or 10 a.m., mainly by factory workers and others who rise early. The midday meal (*Mittagessen*) is the largest and most important of the day. It generally consists of a meat dish

Gingerbread house

One of Germany's best-known foods is gingerbread. The gingerbread house is a very German treat that has appeared in children's tales such as 'Hansel and Gretel'.

For the gingerbread:
6 teaspoons golden syrup
6 teaspoons black treacle
25 g (1 oz) light soft brown sugar
50 g (2 oz) butter
175 g (6 oz) plain flour
1½ teaspoons ground ginger
½ teaspoon baking powder
1 egg beaten
For the icing:
3 eggwhites
425 g (15 oz) icing sugar

Preheat the oven to 200 °C (400 °F). Put the syrup, treacle, sugar and butter in a saucepan. Heat gently, stirring until it is

melted. Sift the flour and ginger into a bowl, stir the baking powder into the melted mixture and add to flour with enough beaten egg to form a soft dough. Knead on a lightly floured surface until smooth. Roll the dough into 0.5 cm (¼ in) slabs and place on baking sheets. Bake for 8 to 10 minutes.

Once cool, cut the slabs into sections to form the base, sides and roof. Fix in place with the icing. Use the remaining icing to decorate the house with sweets.

as well as potatoes or dumplings, gravy and vegetables. The evening meal (*Abendbrot*) usually features breads and an assortment of cold meats, cheeses and spreads.

Germany's cooking reflects its regional diversity, so there are countless 'typical' German dishes. Notable contributions to the world's cuisine include sausages, sauerkraut (pickled cabbage), potato salad, Black Forest gateau and gingerbread (see recipe opposite).

Raise a stein

A stein is a 1-litre (2-pint) mug. Germans drink an average of 140 litres (31 gallons) of beer per person each year – only the Belgians drink more. Germany's 1290 breweries produce more than 5000 varieties of beer, the largest selection in the world.

Brewing was once undertaken only in monasteries. It later became a respected art, and in 1516, the Duke of Bavaria instituted the German Beer Purity Law to govern the quality of beer. It is the oldest working food law in the world and is still followed by German brewers.

Religion in decline

Germany is home to several religions. The vast majority of Germans are **Christians**, and most officially belong to a church, but attendance has declined over the years. Nevertheless, churches remain wealthy, powerful organizations that are involved in public life and politics. They run kindergartens (playschools), hospitals, nursing homes and training centres, and send aid to developing countries. Christian churches fund this work through church taxes, which the government collects each year from church members. Unless they officially leave the church by writing to the government, all members must pay church tax, whether they attend church or not.

Islam is Germany's second-largest religion, with about 1.7 million members. Turkish and other Mediterranean immigrants established both Islam and Greek Orthodox Christianity in the country. Despite the horrors of the **Holocaust** (see pages 68–9), a **Jewish** population remains in Germany, although its numbers are greatly reduced compared to those of the early 20th century. Before World War Two, Germany was home to about 530,000 Jews. Today, there are only about 54,000.

The Christian population of Germany is divided roughly in half between Catholics and Protestants. The south is predominantly Catholic while the north is mainly Lutheran Protestant.

Oktoberfest

Germany's most famous celebration is probably **Oktoberfest**, the largest beer festival in the world. Held every autumn on the Theresienwiese (Theresa's Fields) in Munich, Bavaria, Oktoberfest attracts more than 7 million visitors. As the picture shows, beer halls fill to bursting with people enjoying steins of beer, sausages and 'oom-pah' band music.

The sixteen days of celebration end on the first Sunday in October – hence the name. The festival dates from 12 October 1810, when Munich's citizens celebrated a royal wedding. The event included horse races that were repeated the next year, giving rise to the tradition of Oktoberfest. The horse races no longer take place, but Oktoberfest lives on.

Festivals and celebrations

Germany probably holds more festivals each year than any other country in Europe. Besides the folk festivals that are held in almost every town, the country hosts many international events. Hamburg, for example, has its Ballet Days; Berlin, its International Film Festival. The Bayreuth Festival, staged each summer in Bavaria, is devoted to the performance of Wagner's operas.

Exuberant festivals take place each year in the weeks leading up to Lent. Called *Karneval*, *Fassenacht*, *Fasnet* or *Fasching*, depending on region, these celebrations allow people to have fun before the sombre period of Lent begins. Costumed revellers take part in street parties, and the Rose Monday Parade, part of *Karneval* in Cologne, attracts over a million spectators.

Besides Labour Day (1 May), which honours the workforce, and the Day of Unity (3 October), which celebrates the 1990 reunification, holidays in Germany are of Christian origin. At Pentecost, Christians celebrate the descent of the Holy Spirit. Christmas is a high point of the year. Many well-loved Christmas traditions, including the Christmas tree, originated in Germany. The season begins on the first Sunday after 26 November. Christmas markets are set up throughout the country. The oldest of these markets – the *Christkindlesmarkt* – has been held in Nuremberg every year for more than three and a half centuries. Christmas Eve is the pinnacle of the season, when most families decorate their tree, eat their Christmas meal and exchange gifts.

National holidays

1 January	New Year's Day
March/April	Good Friday
March/April	Easter Sunday
1 May	Labour Day
May/June	Ascension Day
May/June	Pentecost
3 October	Day of Unity
24 December	Christmas Eve
25 December	Christmas Day
26 December	Boxing Day

Shopping

Germany is one of the world's most affluent societies. In the 1970s and 1980s, Germans' love of spending gave rise to large shopping centres and supermarkets on the edges of towns and cities. They competed so successfully against smaller, local shops that many traditional businesses closed. The government has since passed laws limiting the size of stores, but now small local shops face competition from speciality shops and boutiques.

Shopping is governed by a controversial law passed in the 1950s to protect retail workers. It demands that almost all shops close by 6:30 p.m. on weekdays, by 2 p.m. on Saturday and all day on Sunday. As a result, Germany leads the world in mail-order shopping and in numbers of vending machines. These sell almost any item a shopper may wish to purchase after hours.

HOW GERMANS SPEND THEIR MONEY

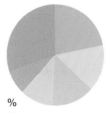

%	
20	food and drink
19	transportation
16	housing
7.3	clothing
4.1	health
6	recreation/culture
27.6	other

source: *Encyclopedia Britannica*

Domestic comforts are important to the Germans. They spend a lot of their money on housing and food.

WHAT DO GERMANS OWN?

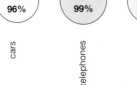

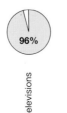

cars	telephones	radios	televisions	refrigerators	washing machines
96%	99%	84%	96%	78%	99%

source: *Encyclopedia Britannica*

The future

'An equal chance to shape one's life in freedom and dignity – that is what we want.'

German politician Oskar Lafontaine

Germany's outlook for the new millennium is very good. Its people have worked hard to overcome the problems of division that existed in the decades following World War Two. They have had to carry the burden of Germany's terrible past. Today, they continue to strive, hoping to overcome the difficulties of reunification.

Germany's role as a constructive, unifying force in European politics has helped the Germans establish a new, positive international identity, one that has helped relieve much of the mistrust that remained in the wake of the **Nazis**. Germany remains a world leader in industry and has a determined, highly educated and skilled workforce that guarantees its future success.

ECONOMIC OVERHAUL

Despite the painful period of adjustment after reunification, Germany's economy still ranks as the third most powerful in the world. Its central geographical position, prime role in the **European Union** (EU) and excellent communications suggest that this will continue.

The government continues to struggle with high unemployment, however, as it works to transform the former **East Germany** into a prosperous, self-sufficient part of the country. Unemployment in Germany peaked at 11.5 per cent in 1997. Companies in the former East Germany continue to close due to restructuring or

Frankfurt's financial centre is one of the main money markets in the world and the investment force behind the regeneration of German industry.

FACT FILE

● In January 2001, Germany was the fifth country in the world for numbers of Internet hosts (organizations ending '.com', '.net' or '.org') behind the USA, Japan, Canada and the UK.

● As a percentage of gross national product (GNP), Germany's spending on health is third in the world, after the USA and Nicaragua.

● Deutsche Bank is Germany's largest bank, with capital of more than £10,885 million. Germany's largest company is Volkswagen, with sales of over £50,000 million. It is closely followed by Siemens and Allianz.

Germans' concerns for their economy are heightened by the emerging trend for large German companies to build their new manufacturing plants in foreign countries. Companies appreciate the German workers' excellent skills, but are reluctant to pay the high wages and benefits they expect.

bankruptcy. The resulting unemployment places a serious drain on Germany's finances in two ways – as long as people remain unemployed, they cannot pay taxes and they also draw social security payments. The government continues to pour hundreds of billions of pounds into upgrading infrastructure, such as transportation, in the former East Germany in order to encourage business investment there.

The amount of hard work and money needed to bring the former East Germany up to par with the **West** took many West Germans by surprise. Many felt resentment and sometimes thought that the East was taking advantage of their hard-won wealth. Germans hope, however, that they can embrace their future together.

CURBING HATE CRIMES

As a free and wealthy Western nation, Germany has gained a reputation as a safe haven, attracting millions of refugees and immigrants from many countries, including Romania, Sri Lanka, Afghanistan, Nigeria and the former USSR. There are strong concerns about the very small group of racists who denounce ethnic minorities, immigrants and refugees. These racists are often termed neo-Nazis (new Nazis).

In 1992, violence was directed at **Jews**, foreign workers and students. Synagogues and refugee homes were fire-bombed, and Jewish graves vandalized. There were more than 1800 separate incidents and eighteen deaths as a result of such attacks. Seeking to curb the growth of racism and extremist groups, many Germans have taken part in massive anti-racism rallies. The government has passed new anti-hate laws banning neo-Nazi groups.

ENVIRONMENTAL CONCERNS

Decades of environmental abuse by German industry and agriculture have raised concerns for the health of humans and wildlife. This pollution is most acute in the former East Germany, where the old **communist** government paid little heed to protecting the environment. One of the worst contributors to pollution is the burning of lignite (brown coal), which was used to produce electricity in the former East Germany. Lignite emissions, along with those from cars, pollute the air and cause **acid rain**, which now threatens to kill large sections of Germany's forests. The destruction of these habitats in turn endangers the wildlife that lives in them.

Poisonous chemicals from air pollution, industrial waste and the herbicides and pesticides used by farmers have made their way into Germany's rivers and lakes. Many urban areas contribute to this pollution problem by releasing raw sewage directly into the waterways. As a result, many of the plants and animals in Germany's rivers and lakes have died. Despite the government's attempts to clean up the water, it will take years to overcome the severe pollution, especially in the eastern part of the country.

> Germany's Green Party was the first environmentalist party to hold seats in a European government. The Greens emerged as a political force in the early 1980s.

German scientists monitor an air pollution research site in Westphalia in north-western Germany.

EUROPEAN UNITY

The EU hopes that economic integration will usher in a period of economic growth, reduced unemployment and greater prosperity for all of its member countries. The adoption in 2002 of the EU's single currency, the euro, as the national currency is considered a major step in building an economic foundation between Germany and other EU members.

Despite their country's upheavals, Germans look forward to positive developments in the new century, with hopes for unity, peace and progress. They look forward to their key role as a major part of the EU and the new economic and political opportunities it promises in Europe and around the world.

Almanac

POLITICAL

country name:
official long form: Federal Republic of
    Germany
short form: Germany
local long form: *Bundesrepublik*
    Deutschland
local short form: *Deutschland*

nationality:
    noun: German(s)
    adjective: German

official language: German

capital city: Berlin

Type of government: federal republic

suffrage (voting rights): everyone
    eighteen years and over

national anthem: 'Deutschlandlied'
    ('Germany's Song')

national holiday: 3 October (German
    Unity Day)

flag:

GEOGRAPHICAL

location: central Europe; latitudes 47°
    to 55° north and longitudes 6°
    to 15° east

climate: temperate

total area: 357,000 sq km
    (137,838 sq miles)
    land: 98%
    water: 2%

coastline: 2389 km (1484 miles)

terrain: lowlands in north, uplands in
    centre, mountains in south

highest point: Zugspitze, 2963 m
    (9721 ft)
lowest point: Freepsum Lake,
    −2 m (−6 ft)

natural resources: coal, iron ore,
    timber, uranium, copper, gas
    and potash

land use:
    arable land: 33%
    forests and woodland: 31%
    permanent pastures: 15%
    permanent crops: 1%
    other: 20%

POPULATION

population (2002 est.): 83.25 million

population density(2000): 235 people
per sq km (609 per sq mile)

population growth rate (2002 est.):
0.26%

birth rate (2002 est.): 8.9 births per
1000 of the population

death rate (2002 est.): 10.4 deaths per
1000 of the population

sex ratio (2002 est.): 96 males per
100 females

total fertility rate (2002 est.): 1.4
children born per woman in
the population

infant mortality rate (2002 est.):
4.65 deaths per 1000 live births

life expectancy at birth (2002 est.):
total population: 77.8 years
male: 74.6 years
female: 81.1 years

literacy:
total population: 99%
male: 99%
female: 99%

ECONOMY

currency: euro (€);
€ 1 = 100 cents

exchange rate (2003):
£1 = € 1.6

gross national product (2000):
£1,320,000 million (third-largest
economy in the world)

average annual growth rate
(1990–99): 1.3%

GNP per capita (2000): £16,094

average annual inflation rate
(1990–2000): 2.4%

unemployment rate (2001): 9.4%

exports (2000): £339,375 million
imports (2000): £294,375 million

foreign aid given (2000): £3450 million

Human Development Index
(an index scaled from 0 to 100 combining statistics
indicating adult literacy, years of schooling, life
expectancy, and income levels):

91.1 (UK 91.8)

TIMELINE – GERMANY

World history

German history

c.50,000 BC

c.40,000 Modern humans – *Homo sapiens sapiens* – emerge

c.800 BC Celtic peoples establish first permanent settlements in Germany

c.100 BC

c.AD 1 Birth of Christ

306 Constantine becomes Roman emperor and Christianity is promoted throughout the Roman empire

c.100 BC German tribes move into northern Europe

AD 9 German tribes under Arminius crush Roman invasion force at Teutoburg

c.AD 400

476 Rome falls to the Goths

c.570 Birth of Muhammad at Mecca

486 Franks under Clovis I conquer Roman territory of Gaul and establish empire in northern Europe

496 Franks convert to Christianity

1545–63 Council of Trent leads to Catholic Church's counterattack against Luther in the Counter-Reformation

c.1350–1550 Italian Renaissance leads to rebirth of the arts and classical learning in Europe

1337–1453 Hundred Years' War between Britain and France

1096 First Crusade to reclaim Jerusalem begins

c.1000 Vikings reach American continent but do not settle

c.AD 800

1618 Beginning of Thirty Years' War

1517 Martin Luther begins the Protestant Reformation

1456 Johannes Gutenberg produces the first printed book in Europe

c.1400

1348 Plague spreads through Germany

1273 Rudolf I becomes first Habsburg Holy Roman Emperor

1241 Hanseatic League is formed, made up of Hamburg, Bremen and Lübeck

c.1200

962 Otto I of the Saxon tribe is crowned Holy Roman Emperor

800 Frankish leader Charlemagne is crowned emperor by the Roman Catholic Church

*c.*1600

c.1750 Industrial Revolution begins in England

1776 American Declaration of Independence

1648 End of Thirty Years' War. Holy Roman empire cedes power to Protestant states

1740 Frederick II becomes king of Prussia and makes it a major power

2000 The West celebrates the Millennium – 2000 years since the birth of Christ

1957 Foundation of the European Economic Community (EEC)

2002 Gerhard Schröder reelected as chancellor

1990 East and West Germany united as single Germany

1989 Berlin Wall comes down

1961 Berlin Wall built

*c.*1780

1789 French Revolution begins

1799 Napoleon Bonaparte becomes emperor of France

1815 Napoleon is defeated at Waterloo

1848 Famine prompts unrest and revolutions throughout Europe

1806 Napoleon conquers Prussia and Austria and dissolves Holy Roman empire

1816 Congress of Vienna establishes German Confederation of 39 states

1862 Bismarck is appointed Prussian prime minister

1866 Prussia defeats Austria and dissolves German Confederation

1871 France is defeated. Germany is created.

1882 Germany forms Triple Alliance with Austria and Italy

*c.*1950

1949 Soviets establish East Germany; Britain, France and the USA establish West Germany

1939 Germany invades Poland

1933 Adolf Hitler is appointed chancellor

1919 Weimar Republic founded

1918 Germany is defeated; Wilhelm II abdicates

1914 Archduke Ferdinand of Austria-Hungary is assassinated, triggering World War One

1945 End of World War Two, defeat of Germany

1939 World War Two begins

1929 Wall Street Crash, beginning of Great Depression

1918 World War One ends

1917 Revolution in Russia leads to establishment of Soviet Union

1914 World War One begins

*c.*1900

Glossary

Abbreviation: Ger. = German

acid rain rain containing damaging pollution

Allies Britain, France, Russia, the USA and other countries that fought together against the Triple Alliance in World War One and the Axis in World War Two

Alpine of the Alps mountains in southern Germany

Basic Law name of Germany's constitution, first adopted by West Germany after World War Two

Bundesrat (Ger.) German parliament's upper house

Bundestag (Ger.) German parliament's lower house

capitalism economic system based on supply and demand, and private ownership of businesses and industry

cathedral large and important church

Christianity religion based on the teachings of Jesus Christ

communism social and political system based on a planned economy in which goods and land are owned by everyone and in which there is no private property

constitution written collection of a country's laws, and its citizens' rights and beliefs

democracy country in which the people choose their government by election, and in which they hold supreme power

East Germany informal name of the former German Democratic Republic, the communist country that existed from 1949 to 1990

export product that is sold to another country

European Union (EU) organization made up of European countries that work together on many economic, social and political issues

foothills lands sloping towards the base of a mountain range

Holocaust planned extermination of European Jews by the Nazis during the period 1941–45

import product that is bought from another country

industrial/ized describes an economy based on developed industries and infrastructure rather than on agriculture

Jew member or descendant of the Hebrew people; a person who practises the religion of Judaism

Land (plural *Länder*, Ger.) organized political unit (state), of which there are sixteen in Germany

Marshall Plan US-sponsored plan to help rebuild western Europe after World War Two through a programme of aid, consisting of loans, food and raw materials

nationalism people's sense of belonging to a nation; also the belief that a nation should be independent of, and sometimes superior to, other nations

Nazi member of the National Socialist German Workers' Party, which controlled Germany from 1933 to 1945 under the dictatorship of Adolf Hitler

Oktoberfest (Ger.) annual beer festival held each autumn in Munich

open market market without tariffs (a charge imposed by government to limit certain types of trade) or other trade barriers

Protestant member of the branch of Christianity that developed from the Reformation and the ideas of Martin Luther. Separate from the Catholic Church in Rome and the authority of the pope

Reformation religious movement begun in 1517 by Martin Luther in an attempt to reform the Catholic Church. The movement led to the founding of Protestantism.

Renaissance great revival of the arts and learning in Europe during the 15th and 16th centuries that built on a rediscovery of the arts of ancient Greece and Rome

republic government in which the citizens of a country hold supreme power and where all citizens are equal under the law

Roman Catholic member of the branch of Christianity based in Rome whose spiritual leader is the pope

socialism political theory that teaches that society as a whole should be in control of a country's resources and businesses

tariff charge imposed by government on imports in order to regulate trade – for example, to protect a country's economy from competition from overseas

totalitarianism type of government in which one political party has complete control under a dictatorship and bans all other political parties

vocational training educational programme that prepares students to perform a trade

West Germany informal name of the former Federal Republic of Germany, the democratic, capitalist country that existed from 1949 to 1990 and which had its capital at Bonn

Bibliography

Major sources used for this book
Ardagh, John, *Germany and the Germans After Reunification* (Penguin, 1991)
The Economist, *Pocket World in Figures* (Profile Books, 2002)
Fulbrook, Mary, *A Concise History of Germany* (Cambridge University Press, 1990)

General further reading
Bennett, Lynda A. (ed.), *Encyclopedia of World Cultures* (G.K. Hall & Co., 1992)
World Reference Atlas (Dorling Kindersley, 2000)
The Kingfisher History Encyclopedia (Kingfisher, 1999)
Student Atlas (Dorling Kindersley, 1998)
The World Book Encyclopedia, (Scott Fetzer Company, 1999)

Further reading about Germany
Bornstein, Jerry, *The Wall Came Tumbling Down: The Berlin Wall and the Fall of Communism* (Portland House, 1990)
Burke, Patrick, *Modern Industrial World: Germany* (Raintree Steck-Vaughn, 1995)
Drews-Bernstein, Charlotte and Garrett, Dan, *World in View: Germany* (Steck-Vaughn Company, 1992)
Library of Nations: Germany, (Time-Life Books, 1984)
Yancey, D. *The Reunification of Germany*, (Lucent Books, 1994)

Some websites about Germany
German Embassy in London
www.germany-embassy.org.uk
The Germany portal
www.deutschland.de/en
German federal government and news site
www.government.de

Index

Acknowledgements

Cover photo credit
Corbis: Peter Turnley

Photo credits
AKG London: 55, 56, 60, 69, 70, 71, 72, 76, 78, 102, 104, Hilbich 108, Erich Lessing 50; **Corbis:** Archivo Iconografico, SA 48, 53, Dave Bartruff 101, Burstein Collection 107, Ric Ergenbright 19, Owen Franken 23, Christel Gerstenberg 65, Naturfoto Honal 28, Wolfgang Kaehler 6, 14, 17, 91, David Lees 58, Christian Liewig 109, Massimo Listri 45, Jim McDonald 46, 87, Sally A. Morgan, Ecoscene 94, Premium Stock 12, Hans Georg Roth 98, Erik Schaffer 31, Gregor Schmid 33, 40, Ted Spiegel 119, Peter Turnley 36, Manfred Vollmer 82, Uwe Walz 21, 29, K. M. Westermann 43, Adam Woolfitt 26, Michael S. Yamashita 25; **Hutchison Library:** Tony Souter 34, 38, 97; **Image Bank:** Hans Wolf 116; **Robert Hunt Library:** 66, 68; **TRIP Photo Library:** M. O'Brien 85, 89, Th-Foto Werbung 37, T. Why 80, Viesti Associates 114

Photo on page 92 courtesy of Volkswagen